HOW TO WIN AT
GOLF

HOW TO WIN AT
GOLF

WITHOUT ACTUALLY
PLAYING WELL

Jon Winokur

Drawings by Kent H. Barton

PAVILION

First published in Great Britain in 2001 by
PAVILION BOOKS LIMITED
London House, Great Eastern Wharf
Parkgate Road, London, SW11 4NQ
www.pavilionbooks.co.uk

Copyright © 2000 by Jon Winokur
Drawings by Kent H. Barton
Design by Johanna Roebas

First Published in the United States by Pantheon Books, a division of
Random House, Inc., New York, and simultaneously in Canada by
Random House of Canada Limited, Toronto.

Pantheon Books and colophon are registered trademarks of
Random House, Inc.

A CIP catalogue record for this book is available from the British
Library.

ISBN 1 86205 545 9

Printed and bound in Spain by Book Print, Barcelona

2   4   6   8   9   7   5   3   1

This book can be ordered direct from the publisher. Please contact the
Marketing Department. But try your bookshop first.

For the original Squires. Except one.

ABOUT THE AUTHOR

Jon Winokur, the author of *The Rich Are Different* and *Advice to Writers,* wants everyone to know that his interest in golfmanship is purely theoretical, and that he would never actually use any of the techniques in this book.

Competitive golf is played mainly on a five-and-a-half-inch course: the space between your ears.

ROBERT TYRE JONES, JR.

You have got to try to think, that guy is your enemy. That is the way competition is. You want to win.

SAM SNEAD

Fitness counts for less in golf than in any other game, luck enters into every minute of the contest, and all play is purely incidental to, and conditioned by, gamesmanship.

STEPHEN POTTER

CONTENTS

FOREWORD

Golf is a cruel game. It is so exacting that even its masters never master it, so intricate that most golfers never achieve consistency. One's command of the swing is so precarious that imperceptible changes in pulse, blood pressure, or body chemistry can ruin everything. You play badly and you don't know why; you play *well* and you don't know why or, worse, you *think* you know why (the golf gods reserve special humiliation for those who think they've discovered the Secret). You strive and struggle, and just when you've made a little progress, golf humbles you yet again.

All golfers, from leading money-winners to Sunday hackers, measure success not by positive accomplishment, but in limiting mistakes: "Don't press, don't dip, don't peek, don't lunge, don't quit, don't sway, don't hook, don't slice, don't shank, etc., etc., etc." Even the scoring system is negative: The object is to achieve the absence of something, i.e., strokes. (In a "B.C." comic strip, a cave woman about to tee off with a crude golf club says to her male companion, "Let me get this straight, the less I hit the ball the better I am doing." "That's right," he replies. "Then why do it at all?" she asks. In the last frame, night has fallen, and the man is still standing there, repeating to himself: "Why . . . do it . . . at . . . all? . . .")

Sad to say, golf excellence is a horizon that recedes as you approach it. The odds are, you'll never reach the point where you're satisfied with your game, and in the unlikely event you do, you'll soon want to play better. And there will lie the seeds of your discontent, because golf isn't cumulative. You don't ratchet yourself upward to ever greater proficiency, you play well one day and poorly the next. You hit one or two or eight or twelve decent shots a round, and many more awful ones.

No, you simply can't play well consistently.

But you can *win* consistently. You cannot master the game, but you can dominate your opponents. Not by outplaying them, by outthinking them.

Golf gamesmen everywhere are indebted to the British satirist Stephen Potter (1900–1969) for the essential vocabulary of the discipline, including, of course, the neologism "gamesmanship." By the time Potter's *Theory and Practice of Gamesmanship*, published in the United States in 1948, had gone through a dozen hardcover printings, the word had found its way into both the English and American lexicons. Potter also published *Lifemanship* and *One-Upmanship* in the 1950s, but it was his seminal *Golfmanship*, published here in 1968, that inspired my own efforts in the field. (Potter called golf "the gamesgame of gamesgames.") Long out of print, *Golfmanship* is Potter at his best: diabolically droll and oh-so-British:

Encyclopaedias and museums can sap, in junior players, the desire to win. If a youth can be made to feel that his match with you is part of a Nordic ritual which has been going on for centuries, it may act as a depressant. The encyclopaedic approach ("first played in 4th century Alexandria"), could dilute, however slightly, the spirit of attack if this fact is first mentioned in a gloomy changing room. Say "Apparently Aubrey writes of the 'games of clout and blatherball'—this would be about 1656." Say this if guest is expecting to be offered a drink. Pictures of Dutch burghers forcing a quoit or disk to slide on ice can make even a scratch player feel momentarily as if he were floundering about in historical gravy. "Curious old print" you can suddenly say to your opponent, in the afternoon round.

Potter relied on the British traditions of amateurism and fair play, so most of his "flurries," "gambits," "hampers," and "ploys" would be lost on contemporary golfers. Hence the present volume, inspired by the principles of golfmanship enunciated by Potter and others, and designed to establish a modern discipline to serve practitioners well into the twenty-first century.*

J.W.
Pacific Palisades

*I welcome feedback from readers, especially suggestions for ploys and gambits. Those with merit will be included in future editions. (Submit to: www.golfmanship.com.)

CAVEATS AND DISCLAIMERS

This book is intended to serve as both a sword and a shield. A sword to attack superior players, a shield to protect against other gamesmen. But if your idea of golf is a few clubs in a canvas bag and the glory of a golden afternoon, if you consider golf a sacrament to be played for the sheer uplift, you won't need it. If, on the other hand, you venture an occasional wager on the game, you have a healthy will to win, and you aren't averse to psychological combat, this book will show you How.

If the Rules of Golf weigh heavily on your conscience, if you're imbued with the lore and tradition of the Royal and Ancient Game, you too need this book, because sooner or later you're bound to come up against a gamesman, and you'll want to know how to defend yourself. And if your idea of gamesmanship is jangling your pocket change or ripping the Velcro on your glove to distract your opponent, you *really* need this book.

In the event you find yourself matched against someone who has apparently also read this book, cease all hostilities immediately. Identify yourselves to each other by means of the code words "Titanic Thompson." Then bow out of the match or, if that isn't possible, reduce the stakes. This will avert an internecine struggle, and you'll both have found a future partner.

The exclusive use of the masculine pronoun throughout is not intended to discourage women from reading and profiting from this book. On the contrary: Most of the techniques are not gender-specific, and a few are even designed to take advantage of male weaknesses (e.g., Ego Play). Nor is it meant to suggest that female opponents should be given more quarter than their male counterparts. An opponent is an opponent regardless of gender, race, or national origin. I just wanted to avoid such awkward locutions as "him or her," "his or hers," "he or she," the even more disagreeable "he/she," and the unthinkable "gamespersonship."

PART I

. . . . .

FUNDAMENTALS
OF GOLFMANSHIP

FIRST PRINCIPLES

1. "Gamesmanship": *Webster's Third New International Dictionary* defines "gamesmanship" as "the art or practice of winning a sports contest by expedients of doubtful propriety (as by distracting an opponent) without actual violation of the rules of the game," and "the art of winning games by cunning or clever practice without actually cheating." Well, yes, but are we not a little harsh in the use of "cunning"? And slightly condescending in the use of "actually"?

However stimulating the moral issues surrounding gamesmanship may be, they're beyond the scope of this book. We shall not concern ourselves with questions of propriety. (Though I would venture that if the editors of *Webster's Third* had been golfers, such a gratuitously prescriptive remark would not appear in their definition.) Suffice to say that golf competition is too important to trust to skill alone, and that gamesmanship, golfmanship, or whatever you care to call it, is a desirable adjunct to one's repertoire of golf shots. For the record, I prefer the first *American Heritage Dictionary* definition: "The art or practice of using tactical maneuvers to further one's aims or better one's position."

2. "Golfmanship": Golf is particularly suited to gamesmanship because of the proximity of the players. As the immortal Potter wrote, "a well-timed failure to smile at an opponent's joke or to react to his sporting gesture is ineffective if the two of you are separated by the length of a tennis court."

3. Your Objective: The sine qua non of winning golf is intense concentration, the ability to stay focused and positive in the face of golf's vicissitudes. Break your opponent's concentration and you destroy his game.

4. Execution: In golf, the harder you try, the worse the results, and the same is true of golfmanship. Ingrain these time-proven techniques, apply them carefully, then relax and trust them to work.

5. "Fairness": Caprice and inconsistency lie at the heart of golfmanship, and a misguided sense of fairness has no place in the value system of the true golfman. Banish your opponent to a shifting landscape and keep him there. If you chafe at the cynicism of such an approach, ask yourself: Is it better to win because you're a great athlete, or because you're an Average Joe who managed to rise above his limitations? Enough casuistry! Is golfmanship unfair? Only if it's done right.

6. The Golfman's Credo: Golf is so difficult, and it is played so badly by so many, often the most effective gambit is to do nothing to alleviate an opponent's distress. Therefore, like the physician, the golfman's credo should be: "First do no harm."

PART II

. . . . .

YOUR OWN
PETARD

SELF-CONTAMINATION

There's nothing more dangerous than a little golfmanship, and nothing more pitiful than a self-styled golfman who defeats himself with his own gambits. To play well it's necessary to spend hours on the practice tee and putting green developing "muscle memory." Well, golfmanship involves a sort of muscle too. Practice these skills until they become second nature—"groove" them, as it were—so their execution is smooth and effortless, and their power is directed exclusively at your opponent.

SELF-DEFENSE

Though the truism "the best defense is a good offense" is the foundation of golfmanship, when an opponent overtly attempts to bother you, retaliate immediately:

Ben Hogan, in his rookie year on Tour, watches a veteran player stand in his putting line on successive holes. Hogan finally warns the offender: "See this putter? If you stand in my line again it's going right between your eyes."

. . .

As I was preparing to hit [during the 1955 Western Open at Portland Golf Club] I saw [Marty] Furgol standing down the fairway between me and the green. I yelled at Doug [Ford] to ask him to move and Doug did, but Marty moved only a few feet. I yelled again, and he moved a couple more feet. With each passing moment I grew hotter and hotter. I swung too hard and the ball flew over the green right, and I should have chipped up for an easy bird, but I missed the putt, too.

Coming off the green I was as mad as I'd ever been on a golf course. I seized Furgol's collar and said to him, "Let me tell you something, Mr. Furgol. If you ever pull a stunt like that again I'll take my fists and beat the hell out of you, and if I can't do it with my fists, I'll use a golf club." ARNOLD PALMER

. . .

Jim Thorpe has a three-shot lead over Jack Nicklaus on the final hole of the '85 Greater Milwaukee Open when Nicklaus asks, "How does it feel to be walking down the last fairway with a three-shot lead over the greatest player to play the game?" Thorpe, equal to the challenge, shoots back, "It feels like you can't win." Thorpe is right.

You must also steel yourself against an opponent's *inadvertent* gamesmanship. If, for example, you're playing someone with a fast swing, take a lesson from Sam Snead, who said that although he liked to play with Ben Hogan because he knew Hogan wouldn't talk much, he never actually watched his swing because, "It was jit-jit—fast back and fast through. I'd watch him address his ball, and when he did his forward press I'd look down the fairway. I'd never watch him swing because I'd get fast, too."

ATTITUDE

. . .

What an individual thinks of himself largely determines what he will do and what he will be. WILLIAM JAMES

A bad attitude is worse than a bad swing.
PAYNE STEWART

. . .

Ever notice that top players seldom make two bogeys in a row and often follow a bogey or double-bogey with a birdie? It's because they put bad play behind them and concentrate on the situation at hand. They stay in the present, they take one shot at a time, they understand that every stroke is equal, and, most important, they don't berate themselves. Adopt the same attitude. Be your own best friend on the golf course. Treat yourself with respect. Even if you're a total bozo.

Your attitude toward your opponent is another matter:

. . .

It is an un-Christian counsel, but the mood for success in golf matches is a silent hatred—temporarily only, be it observed—of your opponent. The genial golfer may be a pleasant fellow to walk round the links with, but his game is all too apt to bear the same resemblance to golf that "bumble-puppy" bears to whist; and worse than that, it tends to produce a similar degeneracy in your own game. Do not, of course, be aggressively rude to an opponent, but do not bother your "dour" mood to make yourself agreeable. All your powers of harming will be needed for your ball. HORACE HUTCHINSON

. . .

"Praise-withholding" is an effective way to express your "silent hatred," and of marshaling your "powers of harming":

Claude Harmon, paired with Ben Hogan in the 1947 Masters, makes a hole-in-one on the 12th. According to legend, as they walk off the green, though the crowd is still applauding in appreciation of the ace, Hogan, who had birdied the hole, asks Harmon, "What did you have?" (Another version has Hogan saying, "Boy, that's the first time I ever birdied that hole!") But Harmon's son Bill recently set the record straight. Hogan actually made a par, he says, and did acknowledge Harmon's ace, albeit grudgingly, muttering something like "Nice shot" as they walked to the 13th tee. Later that evening Harmon asked Hogan why he couldn't have said something more than "Nice shot," and Hogan replied, "Because it wouldn't have helped me a damn bit."

The story bolsters Hogan's dour image, but maybe he was so intent on his own game he didn't notice the second-rarest feat in golf (the double-eagle being the rarest). In any event, the lesson is clear: Harmon had been thinking about Hogan's withholding of praise not just for the rest of the round, but *for years*.

Now, even if you aren't an upbeat person, your game face should not be sullen. Cheerfully acknowledge your opponent's good shots. But don't gush. Be slightly less effusive than he is in response to *your* good shots, and a "compliment gap" will open in his mind. (Likewise, don't actually *laugh* at his jokes, just force a chuckle.) And when your opponent hits his shot-of-the-day, ignore it. Say nothing at all. The silence will gnaw at him.

The obverse, as it were, of praise-withholding is premature or inappropriate praise. I was playing a Los Angeles muni course in a pickup foursome which included an octogenarian who announced on the first tee that he had recently undergone cataract surgery and could not follow the flight of the ball. Throughout the round, it was a mild inconvenience to have to plot the location of his shots for him, and it was disconcerting when he periodically fell into a sort of trance and apparently forgot what he was doing, but the real drag was his habit of exclaiming "Good one!" after my every shot, good or bad. It was especially exasperating on the hole where I pushed my drive onto the adjacent fairway. (Imagine how a touring pro must feel when some imbecile in the crowd yells, "Youdaman!" as he double-crosses a drive, or, "Get in the hole!" as his approach airmails the green.) Anyway, as I trudged through the tree line to find my ball, it dawned on me that the myopic old-timer had unwittingly provided a golfmanship insight: A compliment for a bad shot is a blow upon a bruise.

TANTRUMS If you can endure golf's tribulations with equanimity, it will not only improve your own game, it will also rattle your opponent. Therefore, never throw a club, never swear, never pound the turf in anger after a bad shot. Don't even shake your head in disgust. Your composure under trying circumstances will almost certainly discompose your opponent.

Yes, lose your temper and you'll probably lose the match. It will shatter your concentration and embolden your adversary. But not if you just *pretend*. A feigned temper tantrum can flummox an opponent like nothing else. Just remember that it's an advanced technique fraught with the danger of self-contamination, unless you happen to be a graduate of the Actor's Studio.

Nice touch: Carry a sacrificial club to break over your knee (save the head—the shaft can be replaced again and again).

ATTIRE Though it is better to "play good" than to "look good," the two aren't mutually exclusive. The better you're dressed, the better you feel, and the more you intimidate the opposition. But if your opponent is himself a golf dandy, take the opposite tack and dress down. The more inappropriate your attire, the greater your edge on a man who takes care to turn himself out for a round of golf. As Potter said in another context, "If you can't volley, wear velvet socks."

Note: Black socks with Bermuda shorts are worth a shot a side, minimum.

BAD THINGS HAPPEN TO GOOD GOLFERS (SO IMAGINE WHAT CAN HAPPEN TO YOU)

Even touring pros and top amateurs fail to play their best golf most of the time. They suffer bad bounces, they hit ugly shots, they make mental blunders, and they choke just like you. (Well, not *just* like you.) They run in streaks, seldom post-ing four good rounds in a tournament, because golf is a fickle game. Just when you think you've attained a degree of compe-tence, just when you think it's *safe,* disaster strikes. It's never over until the ball is in the hole, so expect bad things to hap-pen, and never let them faze you. Resist the paranoia of a game that actually does persecute its adherents. Do not succumb to what CBS golf commentator David Feherty calls the "Why Me Syndrome," an affliction that places its sufferers under "the delusion that they receive ten times more bad bounces than does the average golfer."

Conversely, always accentuate the negative for your oppo-nent. Help him fail to rise above his lousy luck. Every time he gets a bad bounce or butchers a shot, keep it fresh in his mind for as long as possible by immersing him in anecdotes of simi-lar disasters. To that end, a catalog of catastrophe from the annals of golf:

In the 1938 U.S. Open at Cherry Hills, Ray Ainsley, a club pro from Ojai, California, after hitting into a stream, decides to play from the water rather than take a penalty. As his ball drifts with the current, he slashes at it repeatedly, stubbornly refusing to take a drop. He finally cards a 19, which is still the U.S. Open record for the highest score on a single hole.

Byron Nelson loses the 1946 U.S. Open when his caddie accidentally kicks his ball.

On the 18th tee in the third round of the 1960 U.S. Open, someone in the gallery clicks a camera at the top of Mike Souchak's backswing. He promptly hooks his drive into a pond, makes double-bogey on the hole, eventually squanders a four-shot lead, and loses to Arnold Palmer.

Roberto De Vicenzo signs an incorrect scorecard at the 1968 Masters and as a result loses the championship by one stroke.

Doug Sanders misses a three-foot putt for the 1970 British Open championship, then loses the playoff to Jack Nicklaus.

In the second round of the 1978 Masters, Japanese professional Tommy Nakajima's fourth shot finds Rae's Creek on the par-5 13th. Electing to hit out of the water rather than take a drop, he pops the ball straight up and it lands on his foot for a two-stroke penalty. When he hands his club to his caddie, it slips from his grasp and falls into the water for another two-stroke penalty. Now lying nine, he chips over the green, then chips back on, then two-putts for a 13, the highest single-hole score in the history of the Masters.

In the 1982 World Series of Golf, Jerry Pate reaches the fringe of a long par-5 in two and faces a fifty-footer for eagle. He rolls his approach five feet past the hole, and his birdie comebacker is also too strong, ending up three feet away. Pate is careless with the par putt and lips it out. He makes an even more careless backhand stab at the bogey tap-in, and not only does it miss the cup, it hits his foot for a two-stroke penalty. He finally holes out for a quadruple-bogey 9.

Hale Irwin loses the 1983 British Open by one stroke when he whiffs a two-inch tap-in.

On a hot day during the 1986 Anheuser-Busch Classic, Billy Kratzert's caddie takes it upon himself to lighten the load by removing all but three balls from the bag. When Kratzert loses them all, he is forced to withdraw from the tournament.

In the 1987 Tournament Players Championship, Raymond Floyd hits a perfect drive on the 11th, but his caddie has left the bag in the fairway and Floyd's ball rolls into it for a two-stroke penalty.

Just as Jeff Sluman is about to strike a five-foot putt on the 17th green in a sudden-death playoff for the 1987 Tournament Players Championship at Sawgrass, a spectator dives into the lake surrounding the green, causing an uproar. Sluman steps away to compose himself, but he misses the putt and loses the playoff to Sandy Lyle on the next hole.

When Bret Ogle tries to thread a two-iron through the trees in the 1990 Australian Open at Royal Melbourne, his ball ricochets off a trunk and breaks his kneecap.

After reaching the 72nd green in the 1992 Las Vegas Invitational, Mark Brooks marks his ball and routinely tosses it to his caddie. The caddie misses it, and the ball rolls into a greenside pond for a one-stroke penalty.

Davis Love III hits his tee shot to within four feet of the cup on the 17th during the 1997 Players Championship, but accidentally brushes the ball with his putter on a practice stroke. He then fails to return the ball to its original position, consequently signs an incorrect scorecard, and is disqualified.

Paul Azinger misses a five-footer for par on the 6th hole in the second round of the 1999 Honda Classic, then misses the tap-in, which lips out and hits his shoe, costing him two more strokes.

After hitting out of a buried lie in a greenside bunker in the second round of the 1999 Bay Hill Invitational, Davis Love III slams his sand wedge into the turf, breaking a sprinkler head, which gushes water and floods the bunker.

THE HORROR

. . .

Sometimes a particular hole will cause a choke—a choke hole. . . . Like the 18th at Cypress. It's like walking into a certain room in a big dark house when you were a kid—you get this fear that hits you. DAVE MARR

. . .

Unfortunately, traumatic golf experiences have a way of resurfacing. Fortunately, such flashbacks can be induced in your opponent. Thus, if he demonstrates a penchant for a particular form of mis-hit (slice, snap hook, shank, cold top, chili dip, etc., etc., etc.), tell him a horror story about a guy you knew who had the same problem, *may he rest in peace.* Or if your opponent seems to have difficulty with a particular hole, convince him that the hole is his nemesis, and the next time he plays it, the negative memories will come flooding back, drowning out any positive thoughts or visualizations.

PLAY IT AS IT LAYS

Joan Didion's novel *Play It As It Lays* has nothing to do with golf, but it does contain something to help you win. The narrator, Maria, after losing everything, reveals what she's learned about Life: "One thing in my defense, not that it matters: I know something Carter never knew, or Helene, or maybe you. I know what 'nothing' means, and keep on playing." Which also applies to golf. (Some would have you believe that golf is a metaphor for life; of course, the reverse is true.) At any rate, the lesson is clear: In golf as in life, you shouldn't kid yourself.

For example, most amateur golfers roll the ball over. That is, they play winter rules all year round. Which is why *you* should insist on playing the ball "down" (i.e., "as it lays") whenever conditions reasonably permit. This will give you an advantage over your opponent, who's probably among the legion of golfers who routinely touch the ball. Forced to play it down, he'll suddenly have to hit from a variety of unfamiliar lies, but you won't have to adjust. And there's another potential dividend: the chance that your opponent, accustomed to moving the ball, will absent-mindedly nudge it with the club-head and incur a one-stroke penalty.

Playing the ball down will teach you how to play all kinds of shots from all kinds of lies, and your overall game will benefit. But be clear: Your motive for playing it as it lays is not to improve your ball-striking, or to uphold the purity of the game, but to give you an edge.

CLUB RECONNAISSANCE

. . .

You can't hit a good five-iron if you're thinking about a six-iron on your backswing. CHARLES COODY

. . .

Club selection is a crucial aspect of the game:

During the Western Open at Medinah in the 1960s, Dave Marr and Sam Snead reach the par-3 14th. Marr, with the honor, catches Snead straining to see what club he's about to hit—Marr later says the shot was a six-iron for him and a seven for Snead. Marr selects a four-iron and "dead hands" the shot—i.e., he hits a high, floating ball that lands softly on the putting surface. Snead promptly pulls a six-iron and airmails the green. "The ball was still rising when it went over the gallery," said Marr. "If looks could have killed, the one that Sam gave me would have planted me right on the tee."

Marr's counter to Snead's club reconnaissance is not offered as an affirmative technique—if you had that much control

1. INCORRECT.   2. CORRECT.

CLUB RECONNAISSANCE: Experienced players automatically conceal the clubhead with their hand as they pull an iron from the bag (and good caddies do the same).

over the ball, you probably wouldn't be reading this book—but rather as a defense against an opponent who tries to mislead you.

In a 1971 Ryder Cup match, Bernard Gallacher's caddie asks Arnold Palmer what club he hit on a par-3 and Palmer tells him. A match official overhears the exchange and awards Palmer the hole.

Seeking an opponent's advice, including asking what club he hit or plans to hit on a given shot, is a breach of the rules punishable by loss of hole in match play and two strokes in medal play. It's also a tacit admission of weakness. (Some would maintain that you don't want to know anyway, because swings are too varied for the information to be of much use. One man's three-wood is another man's five-iron.)

It is better, of course, to know yourself what to hit without having to rely on your opponent. Which is why you should "dial in" your clubs on the practice range. Determine how far you carry each one. If you still doubt what to use on a given shot, err on the side of too much club. Remember that water and elevated greens require more "carry" and hence more club, and factor in other conditions such as wind, firmness of greens, even your own "adrenaline."

On the other hand, if your opponent asks you what club *you* hit, or comes right out and asks for a recommendation, he has delivered himself into your hands:

Low road: Call him on the rule and assess the penalty.

High road: Don't call him on the rule, but try to mis-club him.

Walter Hagen and Al Watrous are tied in the 1925 PGA Championship at Olympia Fields. With their drives on the dangerous 18th, a long par-5 with water fronting the green, Hagen finds the left rough and Watrous, who's in good shape in the fairway, decides to lay up with an iron, but glances over to see Hagen taking practice swings with a wood. Figuring that if Hagen is going for the green he'd better do likewise, Watrous switches to a wood and promptly hits into the water. Whereupon Hagen goes back to the iron he'd planned to use all along, plays safe down the fairway, and makes a routine par to win the match.

There are various countermeasures for a "bag hawk":

- If your and your opponent's prospective shots are about the same distance (either from the tee on a par-3 or from the fairway on a par-4 or -5,) and he's first to play, try Hagen's tactic: Immediately select your club—the wrong club—then, after he hits his shot too long or too short, "change your mind" and pull the right one.
- Audibly ask your caddie for a five-iron while taking a six (or a four).
- Switch the headcovers on your metal woods periodically so only your caddie knows for sure.

• Always conceal the clubhead with your hand as you pull an iron from the bag.

Note: Do not go to the extreme of changing the lofts on your clubs by bending your three-iron into a two, your four-iron into a three, etc. It's an unnecessary job of manual labor given the simple alternatives already cited.

. . . . .

PART III

KNOW
YOUR ENEMY

SPECIAL CASES

In the three-man playoff in the 1913 U.S. Open at the Country Club in Brookline, Massachusetts, Harry Vardon and Ted Ray are the leading professionals in the world, and Francis Ouimet is an obscure, twenty-year-old amateur with a ten-year-old caddie. But Ouimet leads Vardon by a single stroke after twelve holes. On the 13th tee, Vardon takes out a cigarette, and Ouimet notices that his hands shake when he lights it. Which, Ouimet later reveals, gives him the confidence he needs: He finishes strong, shooting a 2-under-par 72 (to Vardon's 77 and Ray's 78) to win the national championship.

Sam Snead studied opponents the way Ted Williams studied pitchers, always searching for weakness. Snead looked for signs of fear in the eyes (enlarged pupils), on the lips (whiteness), and in the putting stroke (generally the first part of the game to succumb to nerves). A sudden change in mannerisms was another key for Snead. If fast walkers slowed down, or slow walkers sped up, Snead read vulnerability. Thus when he played Jim Turnesa in the finals of the 1942 PGA Championship and Turnesa made two more waggles than usual on the 10th tee, Snead knew Turnesa was getting tight, which gave him added confidence. He won 2 and 1.

Try to detect weakness in *your* opponents. "Tells" include indecision on club selection, difficulty breathing, frequent yawning (internal stress robs the body of oxygen), increased chatter, and temper tantrums which, according to Snead, are disastrous.

BEGINNERS With the explosive growth of the game, there will be many new golfers uninitiated not only in the rules and etiquette of golf, but also in the "country club scene" with its attendant social graces. These nouveau golfers have the additional burden of being in constant apprehension of committing faux pas. If you find yourself playing such a parvenu, by all means take advantage of his insecurity by calling attention to his every lapse, and perhaps even inventing a few rules of your own.

LEFTIES Left-handers present a special opportunity. First, remember that they're accustomed to discrimination: The word "sinister"—ominous, baleful, malign—comes from a Latin root meaning "the left side." Which reflects the mind-set of societies since time immemorial. To this day, in many cultures left-handed children are "cured" by being made to do everything right-handed, and until recently—perhaps because of the emergence of Phil Mickelson—left-handed golfers were "turned around" and made to play right-handed.

Thus in a match with a southpaw, prey upon his lifelong sense of alienation by quoting a "study" showing that left-handed golfers are at a distinct disadvantage because of the "right-hand bias of golf course architects." Conversely, if your opponent is one of those lefties who plays right-handed, shake his confidence by asking whether he ever thought he'd play better from his "natural" side. (This is special pleading—and golfmanship—at its finest.)

NEGAHOLICS In my youth, I had the misfortune of playing frequently with a fellow named Richard who scolded himself. Whenever he missed a shot, he would shout, "God Almighty, Dick!" Which, I think, gave him a twofold edge: (1) it filled the air with negativity, and (2) it caused his more thoughtful opponents to ruminate on whether God ought to be involved in the first place. Richard was a classic "neggie," and they're not as easy to handle as you might think. They fume and sputter, they curse every shot, they berate themselves for their mistakes. But they also contaminate the atmosphere, and if you're not careful, they'll drag you down with them, so you'll have to inure yourself to their pestilent outbursts before you can help them self-destruct.

THE HANDICAPPED In the spirit of the times, which rightfully treats the handicapped as "challenged" but equal, do not insult your physically handicapped opponent by showing him mercy.

THE AURALLY SENSITIVE There's an old chestnut about a golfer whose concentration is so fragile that he's disturbed by a butterfly two fairways over, flapping its wings on his backswing. An exaggeration, of course, but there are golfers who cannot abide noise. Though a golf course is generally thought to be a quiet refuge from the din of modern life, it can be quite noisy, what with cart backup alarms, tractors, sprinklers, mowers, chain saws, etc.

If your opponent betrays an aural sensitivity, make sure to call his attention to all the distracting noises, then take him aside and point out that it's silly to be disturbed by them. Tell him: "After all, even if you could create a perfectly controlled, absolutely noiseless environment to play in, there'd still be the sound of your own pulse throbbing in your ears."

CELL PHONE USERS

. . .

The first time at Osprey Ridge, I played with three young radiologists from the Orlando area. One of the radiologists had a beeper in his pocket, and he stopped several times during the round to talk to patients on a cellular phone that he kept beside him on the seat in his golf cart. He would say, "Just a minute, I have to check your file." Then he would put the phone on hold and hit his ball.
DAVID OWEN

. . .

It rankles me to see someone using a cellular telephone in public, especially when they're behind the wheel of a car (Hang up and drive!), in a restaurant (You're not that important!), or walking down the street (Watch where you're going!). But the worst place is on a golf course. To me, there's nothing more antithetical to the pastoral game than the sight of a ponytailed baby mogul with a Cohiba in his kisser and a flip phone in his ear. No wonder a growing number of courses ban cell phones, and some clubs fine or suspend members who use them on the property. I therefore strongly urge you to leave your phone at home.

But . . . if you must: Arrange to have someone call you at an appointed time. Obviously, receiving calls or pages is a two-edged sword: It can distract you as well as your opponent, so if the match is going in your favor, turn the phone off; if the match is going against you, raise the volume on the ringer.

Hitting DIAL TONE as your opponent makes his backswing is not recommended, but placing a call to check on something at the office (or to confirm that your dry cleaning is ready) is more worthy of a true golfman and would infuriate anyone. Arranging a golf lesson is a nicer touch, as is confirming a future tee time with someone else.

Defense: If you find yourself matched against someone with a cell phone or pager, there are various countermeasures, including simply asking him to leave it in his locker. But perhaps the most effective approach is to turn it into an instrument of torture for him: Find out the number and have someone call and hang up repeatedly, or put him on terminal hold, or pretend to be a telemarketer. In a less elaborate approach, has he seen the article in the *New England Journal of Medicine* about the link between cell phone use and brain cancer?

Note: As of this writing, the U.S. stock market is riding high. Rampant speculation, especially in technology stocks, is being fueled by online day-trading. People who don't know a put from a putt are carrying pagers that beep when a given stock hits a target price. Let's hope that by the time you read this the market will have corrected and these people will no longer be able to afford to play golf.

CHEATERS

. . .

Golf is the hardest game in the world to play and the easiest to cheat at.   DAVE HILL

Golfers who claim they never cheat also lie.
HENRY BEARD

. . .

Professional golf is a bastion of civility in a world of trash-talking ath-a-letes. It's an honor-system sport in which competitors police themselves. The standard was set by the great Bobby Jones, who said, after being congratulated for penalizing himself for an infraction only he knew about: "You might as well praise a man for not robbing a bank."

Alas, this attitude is increasingly rare. In a recent survey of American business executives, 70 percent said they play golf to win, and over 50 percent said they wanted to win badly enough to have cheated at least once. Let's be crystal clear: We're talking about cheating, not merely breaking the rules.

Breaking the rules can be unintentional. Cheating is deliberate and premeditated.

CHEATING AND GOLFMANSHIP Potter's *Theory and Practice of Gamesmanship* is subtitled *The Art of Winning Games Without Actually Cheating.* Indeed, it is axiomatic that cheating has no place in golfmanship. Cheating is coarse and dishonest and, more important, being labeled a cheater at golf is the kiss of death. Nobody wants to play with you. And you can't win if you don't play. Therefore, cheating as a tactic will not be countenanced in this book. (It could, of course, be the subject of another book, but such an enterprise would almost certainly be repugnant to this author.)

Cheating is to golfmanship what butchery is to neurosurgery, armed robbery is to salesmanship, croquet is to golf. Which is to say it is crude, unseemly, and beneath the dignity of a serious person. But golfmanship, practiced well, is an art.

The golfman never cheats. Rather, he is the mongoose to the cobra, battling cheaters with skill and ferocity, meting out swift justice.

CAUTIONARY TALES
True story: A foursome is playing an uphill par-3 with a blind tee shot. Golfer A fires at the flag but fears it is too strong, and sure enough, when he arrives at the green, his ball is nowhere to be found. He combs the deep rough behind the green but still can't locate it, so he furtively drops a second ball and pretends it's his tee

shot. He then chips to within gimme range for a "par." When golfer B holes out, he discovers golfer A's first ball in the cup.

CHARGED GOLF CHEAT "ROTTING IN JAIL"

INDIANAPOLIS—Charles Carey says he's "rotting in jail" three weeks after he was arrested for allegedly cheating on his score during a charity golf tournament.

"It's been like living in Nazi Germany here," Carey said by telephone from the Hamilton County jail, where he has been since his Sept. 30 arrest. "Things are getting worse and worse. I haven't been convicted of anything."

The 47-year-old from Thorntown is charged with theft for allegedly shaving at least 13 strokes from his score to better his chances of winning a tournament.

Sheriff's detectives, responding to a tip, say they followed Carey during his round at Hanging Tree Golf Club. Carey claimed he shot a 67, won second place and a $50 gift certificate.

Carey was arrested in the parking lot after accepting his prize.

A Dec. 2 pretrial hearing on the theft charge has been set. If convicted, Carey could be sentenced to a maximum fine of $10,000 and three years in prison.

Palm Beach Post, October 20, 1993

The good news for Mr. Carey: The cheating charges were dropped. The bad news: They were dropped because he was extradited to Colorado on a forgery rap.

CHEATING AMONG THE PROS Most touring pros are scrupulous about calling inadvertent violations on themselves, as when the ball moves at address, or when they accidentally ground the club in a hazard. Typically, the player will assess the penalty on himself, then, in the Bobby Jones tradition, modestly insist that anyone would have done the same because "that's the rule." Otherwise, it's virtually impossible for touring pros to cheat. They're under constant scrutiny not only from fellow competitors and tournament officials, but also from attentive galleries and couchbound duffers monitoring their every move on television. As a result, cheating incidents on the pro tours are conspicuous by their rarity:

Greg Norman accuses Masashi "Jumbo" Ozaki of improving his lie in the fairway during a tournament in Japan. No penalty is called, perhaps because of the home course advantage, and Ozaki goes on to shoot 67 to Norman's 70.

Ken Green calls Raymond Floyd a "dirtball" and accuses him of cheating in the 1983 Doral Open, but no official action results.

Vijay Singh is accused of signing an incorrect scorecard in a tournament in Indonesia in 1983. He is suspended from the Asian tour for two years but steadfastly maintains it was a scorekeeper's error.

Tom Watson, who wrote a book on the rules of golf, accuses Gary Player (whom he calls "the little man") of uprooting a leaf that obstructed him on the 16th hole of the 1983 Skins Game. Player insists he didn't move the leaf but merely examined it. Player later demands that Watson relinquish his 1977 Masters and British Open titles because the grooves on his clubs were subsequently ruled illegal.

A TV viewer calls in to accuse Hale Irwin of cheating during the second round of the 1990 U.S. Open by rolling his ball along the green in violation of the rule that prohibits testing the putting surface. No one else sees the alleged infraction and no action is taken against Irwin.

After the first round of the 1995 World Series of Golf, Greg Norman accuses Mark McCumber of cheating by tamping down a spike mark. McCumber maintains he was only brushing away an insect, but Norman refuses to sign McCumber's scorecard, briefly threatens to leave the tournament, then goes on to win it. No action is taken against McCumber by the PGA Tour.

Tom Watson addressed the issue of cheating on the Tour at a banquet in his honor during the 1996 Australian Masters: "There is no question that people cheat on the tour," he said. "The game is a game of integrity, but you are talking about money and you're talking about livelihoods." He refused to name names, saying only: "We know who they are."

Defense against cheaters: To paraphrase the old adage, "Keep your partners close and your opponents closer." If you suspect something, watch your opponent's every move and let him *know* he's being watched. This will yield a double benefit: He'll be aware of the scrutiny and perhaps be distracted by it, and he'll be nervous about inadvertently breaking the rules, let alone cheating. But ultimately there's only one way to deal with a confirmed cheater: Never play with him again.

Forewarned is forearmed. Here are a few of the cheater types you may encounter.

"The Improver"

. . .

He who have fastest cart never have to play bad lie.
MICKEY MANTLE

. . .

This guy rushes to his ball and improves his lie, either before his opponent arrives, or while everyone else is watching someone hit (all eyes are naturally drawn to a ball in flight). Or he'll bend down, ostensibly to move debris from around his ball, and deftly nudge it into a better lie. Or pretend to inspect the ball to "identify" it, improving the lie in the process. Some will actually place the ball on a tee if left unsupervised long enough. Careful surveillance is thus the only effective counter-measure against the Improver.

"The Accountant"

The Accountant can't keep track of all his strokes.

. . .

I used to play golf with a guy who cheated so badly that he once had a hole in one and wrote down a zero on the scorecard. BOB BRUE

. . .

The Accountant should be audited on every hole.

"The Mechanic"

This individual illegally modifies the grooves on his irons to make the ball stop more quickly on the green. Or uses a souped-up ball. Or drills holes in his driver to infuse it with mercury. The surest way to defeat a mechanic is by exposing and disqualifying his doctored equipment.

"The Ball Hawk"

When the Ball Hawk loses his ball in the woods, he simply drops another. "Here it is!" he shouts. Some ball hawks have a hole in the pants pocket for discreet dropping.

How to handle a ball hawk? An effective albeit elaborate method is detailed in *Goldfinger* (1964). British secret agent James Bond (Sean Connery) is assigned to bring down Auric Goldfinger (Gert Fröbe), an international master criminal who loves gold and golf. When Bond drops an ingot worth £5,000 on the practice green in front of Goldfinger, the game is on.

Cut to the back nine: With the match all square, Goldfinger loses his drive in the rough. Oddjob (Harold Sakata), Goldfinger's Korean manservant-bodyguard-caddie (with the lethal derby), furtively drops a second ball through his pants leg. Bond sees it, as does his caddie, who says, "If that's 'is ball, I'm Arnold Palmer." To which Bond replies, "T'isn't." "How d'ya know?" asks the caddie. "I'm standing on it," says Bond.

Bond slips the ball into his pocket, allowing Goldfinger to play the second ball. Goldfinger makes a 5 to Bond's 6 and wins the hole. Ever the sportsman, Bond obligingly retrieves Goldfinger's ball from the cup, but in the process replaces it with another one. Goldfinger then tees off with it on the 18th without detecting the switch, holes out, and thinks he's won the match. Bond again retrieves the ball from the cup and "notices" it isn't Goldfinger's, assesses the penalty—loss of hole for playing the wrong ball—and wins the match and the bet.

When playing someone who can miraculously find a lost ball no matter how deep in the woods (as long as it's his), keep a close watch, and enforce the five-minute rule. The James Bond switch should be considered an advanced technique.

"The Caddie/Ball Hawk"

Some people seem to think caddies are to cheating what real estate brokers are to selling your house: You might be able to manage without them, but it's worth the price to let them do the dirty work.

"Picasso"

Picasso carries a can of white spray paint in his bag to illegally draw a circle around his ball when no one is looking. (A white circle indicates "ground under repair" and affords a free drop.) If you catch Picasso in the act, walk up to him, seize his spray can, rip off the valve as if stripping the epaulet from the shoulder of a disgraced officer, look him in the eye, and growl: "I may not know much about art, but I know what I don't like!"

"The Inchworm"

This player illegally marks his ball to avoid a spike mark or to get closer to the hole. Inchworming is probably the most common form of cheating because it's virtually undetectable. It's certainly the most common form of alleged cheating by touring pros:

> Bob Toski withdraws from the Senior Tour in 1986 in the wake of inchworming charges, and Jane Blalock is suspended by the LPGA in 1972 for the same reason. Blalock had been Toski's student, and when told of her suspension Toski says she probably slipped into the habit "subconsciously."

> During the 1997 Trophée Lancôme, Swedish pro Jarmo Sandelin accuses Mark O'Meara of inchworming by marking his ball and then replacing it a few centimeters closer to the hole. O'Meara wins the title and denies

wrongful intent. A year later in the same tournament, Lee Westwood accuses Sandelin of grounding his putter behind the ball and causing it to move. Sandelin insists he hadn't grounded it, though he admits the ball moved.

I witnessed a flagrant form of inchworming at a tournament in Las Vegas some years ago. My foursome included the entertainer Peter Lind Hayes, a retired oral surgeon from St. Louis, and a local resident who, when marking his ball with a quarter, would kneel down, flip the coin several feet toward the hole, pick up his ball, and then, when it was his turn to putt, replace the ball at the closer point. (This wasn't inchworming, this was grasshoppering.) Needless to say I was taken aback, not only by the flipping, but also because no one challenged the man. Then my caddie clued me in: The offender was the reputed head of a well-known but illegal family business. As it happened, our group finished out of the money, so, no harm no foul, I chose not to take the fellow to task.

"The Greaser"

It may come as a shock to gentle readers, but despite the rule prohibiting the application of foreign substances, the Greaser smears Chapstick or Vaseline on his clubs. Grease takes sidespin off the ball, preventing it from hooking or slicing, and makes it fly farther. There's even an over-the-counter product for the purpose called GoGrease. Do the pros grease up? Probably not, but one popular Tour star has been accused of rubbing his driver on his own cheek to get the same effect.

When you suspect you're playing a greaser—and it's hard to catch one in the act—look for the telltale signs: Blades of grass and dead insects tend to stick to the faces of his irons, and he never wants to shake your hand.

"The Poocher"

The Poocher doesn't just roll the ball over to improve his lie, he actually uses a club to dig up a small mound of turf so the ball *really* sits up. This vile practice was a criminal offense in Scotland until 1934. Lee Trevino has been known to legally use it, sometimes called a "chopita," on par-3s (though most authorities urge the use of a tee whenever permissible). What to do if you encounter a poocher? Resist the urge to dig up a small mound of turf from his scalp.

CHOKERS

. . .

Golf is a choke game. Nobody ever shanked a three-iron because his opponent threw him a curve or put too much topspin on the ball. When Scott Hoch missed a three-foot putt to blow the 1989 Masters, the ball was sitting perfectly still when he hit it and the crowd was perfectly silent. It was completely, entirely, totally him. That's why golf is also the cruelest game.

MARK MULVOY

I don't deny I'm nervous. I have always maintained that a man who is not nervous is either an idiot or has never been close enough to winning to get nervous.
CARY MIDDLECOFF

For an amateur, standing on the first hole of the Masters is the ultimate laxative. TREVOR HOMER

. . .

The *American Heritage Dictionary* defines "choking" as "the failure to perform effectively because of nervous agitation or tension." A gross understatement to anyone who has ever yipped an eighteen-incher for All the Money.

Sports psychologist Bob Rotella dislikes the word "choke." He prefers "getting in the way of your performance." And in most circles it's considered downright rude to accuse someone of choking, hence the many euphemisms, including "gag," "lump," "the apple," "the pressure goiter," "take the pipe," "swallow the olive," "gargle peanut butter," etc., etc., etc.

Never think you're the only one with first-tee palsy or the tendency to choke over a short putt. Everyone gets the jitters, and your opponents suffer from them at least as much as you do. Even touring pros have problems. Some are rumored to use prescription drugs to keep anxiety under control, and a few have actually admitted feeling pressure, as when Larry Mize confessed that when he's in the lead he gets butterflies in his stomach and just hopes they're "flying in formation." Sandra Haynie, asked to describe the biggest improvement in her game after twenty years, replied, "I don't throw up." After winning the 1981 PGA Championship, Larry Nelson told reporters, "My biggest concern was that I would come to the 18th hole with a one-shot lead and choke. I'm a choker." Gary Player said the pressure gets worse as he gets older: "The hole begins to look like a Bayer aspirin." And Tom Watson summed it up: "We all choke. You just try to choke last."

So the next time you get the dry mouth or the lump in the throat, console yourself with the knowledge that you're just like everybody else, including the greats, and—more important—your opponent.

Golf is such a precarious game, and our grasp of its complex skills is so tenuous, most of us are constantly battling our fear of failure. Your task is to reinforce your opponent's fear by cultivating the seeds of self-doubt already growing in his fragile psyche, and thus helping him choke early and often:

High road: When your opponent chokes, it is sometimes to your benefit not to acknowledge it. That way he can forget about it as quickly as possible and never address the problem.

Low road: If you play in a jovial foursome, after your opponent chokes, say on a short putt, approach him from behind, place your arms around his midsection with the hands slightly above the solar plexus and employ a firm upward thrust. When he recoils in astonishment, tell him it's okay, you're just administering the Heimlich maneuver.

Another species of choking occurs when a golfer plays over his head for several holes and then wakes up. When playing someone who expects to make bogeys but suddenly finds himself under par, accentuate his discomfort by remarking how unusually *well* he's playing, and by reminding him that all he needs is to *par in* (or whatever) for his *personal best* (or whatever).

Legend has Dean Martin on the 18th green at Riviera facing a ten-footer for $10,000. Just as he is about to stroke the ball, his opponent says, "Don't choke!" Dino looks up and replies, "How can you choke for ten thousand when you're worth fifty million?" and promptly drains the putt.

· · ·

Everyone has his own choking level, a level at which he fails to play his normal golf. As you get more experienced, your choking level rises. JOHNNY MILLER

· · ·

Before he became a drug-addled, microphobic recluse who wore Kleenex boxes as bedroom slippers, the billionaire Howard Hughes was a scratch golfer who once played in the U.S. Amateur. Hughes regularly beat better players simply by raising the stakes until they reached their "choking level."

Lesson: Do not play for more money than you can afford to lose. Better yet, don't play for more than you have in your pocket. And don't carry a lot of cash.

PLAYING-THROUGH SYNDROME There's a tendency to rush when "playing through" a slower group. Normal performance anxiety is magnified by the realization that these people have just done you a favor (yielding to a faster group is perhaps the ultimate courtesy in a courtly game) and you feel obligated. The tendency is to *appear* to hurry so as not to seem ungrateful by taking too much time. Which makes you careless. Then there are the obligatory professions of gratitude as you hole out and hustle off the green, and the standard "We'll get out of your way." Do not succumb to Playing-Through Syndrome. Understand that nobody cares a whit about your game, so take your time and make a solid stroke. Your aplomb under the circumstances will add to your opponent's distress.

BOOZERS

. . .

Tension in the arm muscles ruins golf swings, most often promoting a slice. Almost anything that causes a golfer to squeeze his club harder will ruin his game; conversely, almost anything that causes a golfer to ease up on his death grip will improve his accuracy and length. Hence, beer. A moderate infusion of alcohol can have the same effect on the muscles of golfers that it is said to have on the inhibitions of attractive strangers in bars. That is why golfers sometimes refer to alcoholic beverages as "swing oil." DAVID OWEN

. . .

Many golfers believe alcohol enhances performance by soothing nerves, relaxing muscles, and bolstering confidence. Hence the popularity of the roving beverage cart. In fact, alcohol depresses the central nervous system, impairs balance, and disrupts hand-eye coordination. Even a small amount consumed just before or during a round will have a negative effect on your ability to think clearly and perform golf's complex psychomotor skills. Alcohol is also a diuretic, so the more beer you drink on a hot day, the more dehydrated you become. Even a shot of whiskey on a chilly afternoon has the opposite of the intended effect: Alcohol causes the blood vessels in your skin to dilate, resulting in *loss* of body heat.

You should therefore eschew alcohol as a means of enhancing your game. And encourage your opponent to consume as much as possible.

SHANKERS

A shank occurs when the ball is struck on the hosel or neck of the club, causing it to fly ninety degrees to the right of the target. It's the result of taking the club too far inside on the backswing. Or it may stem from keeping the weight on the toes during the downswing, or by standing too close to the ball at address, or by dipping the upper body toward the ball. Or all of the above. Or some of the above. Or none of the above.

Whatever its cause, the shank is universally feared as the most lethal, most demoralizing, most revolting swing disease—the flesh-eating virus of golf. It strikes without warning and no one is immune, not even world-class players:

In the 1985 U.S. Open at Oakland Hills, T. C. Chen, a twenty-five-year-old touring pro from Taiwan, leads by four shots after fifty-eight holes, having scored the only double-eagle in the history of the U.S. Open in the first round. After driving his ball safely onto the 5th fairway, he shanks his second shot. He is so unnerved—he had played flawless golf to this point—he commits the now infamous "double hit." He cards a quadruple-bogey 8, bogeys the next three holes, loses the championship to Andy North by one stroke, and is forever saddled with the nickname "Two Chips Chen."

Mark Calcavecchia is dormie four over Colin Montgomerie in the 1991 Ryder Cup. He loses the 15th and 16th, and at the par-3 17th, after Montgomerie puts his tee shot into the water and all Calcavecchia has to do is hit his ball somewhere on dry land, he shanks it into the water, then misses a two-foot putt, allowing Montgomerie to halve the match. (Fortunately for Calcavecchia's subsequent mental health, the American team wins anyway.)

"Shank" is to golfers what *Macbeth* is to actors: It is considered bad form to utter the word. Hence the variety of euphemisms, including: "squirter," "lateral," "snap fade," "power push," "pitch out," "El Hosél," "the shot that dare not speak its name," and the Cockney rhyming slang, "merchant bank," "Sherman Tank," and "J. Arthur" (short for "J. Arthur Rank").

When a golfer suffers a shank during a round, silent panic spreads through the foursome, as if the victim has just coughed up blood. Having the shanks is a vicious cycle: If you tend to shank, you lose confidence, the lack of confidence makes you tentative, and the tentativeness promotes more shanks. (It has thus been suggested that the toughest shot in golf is the one immediately after a shank.) And the shanks leave as suddenly and mysteriously as they arrive, which only heightens their terrible specter.

Every golfer has at least one shank horror story (a redundancy) and many have a pet cure the way folks have home remedies for the common cold. There's even a theory that the shank is close to a perfect shot, a notion with a monumental implication: If the ugliest shot in golf is next to perfection, the game is even more insidious than we imagined.

If your opponent is prone to shanking, you'll of course have a tremendous edge. The primary gambit is to make sure he never quite forgets his affliction. Thus if he's playing a shank-free round and should happen to flush an iron, remark, "Looks like you've cured your shank!" If he's been shanking all day but finally manages to hit a solid shot, exclaim, "Whoa, *that* one wasn't on the hosel!" And when you're behind in the match, remind him even more overtly: Actually saying the word would be seen as a bald provocation, so pretend to almost slip—get the "sh" out and then stop yourself. You'll have said it without saying it.

Caution: When playing a shanker, never watch him swing.

THE SUPERSTITIOUS

Jack Nicklaus never plays a round of golf without three pennies in his pocket: one to mark his ball, a second in case he loses the first, and a third in the event somebody needs to borrow one. And he marks with the tails side up. Justin Leonard always uses a coin minted in the sixties—to remind him of the score he is trying to shoot. During LPGA tournaments, Karrie Webb uses a number-four ball on Thursday, a three on Friday, a two on Saturday, and a one on Sunday. Ben Crenshaw won't use a ball with a number higher than four, the maximum score he's prepared to take on any given hole. Indeed, most touring pros shun high-numbered balls. Some don't even like number-three balls (bad juju: three-putt). Some never take a birdie ball out of play, even if it's damaged.

Tom Weiskopf likes to use a broken tee on par-3s, but Nancy Lopez won't touch one. The late Bert Yancey always stayed with a family named Masters during the annual tournament at Augusta National, and when playing there Charles Coody always goes to bed precisely twelve hours before his tee time the next day, even if it means turning in at 9:12 P.M. Before the first round of the Players Championship at Sawgrass, Gary Player ritually "sacrificed" four balls into the water surrounding the 17th green to inoculate himself against disaster.

As he enters the 18th tee box with a one-stroke lead over Jack Nicklaus in the final round of the 1970 British Open, Doug Sanders is accosted by a spectator who hands him a white tee and says: "This tee was used by Tony Lema in the 1964 Open. Use it for luck." Seeing no harm, Sanders uses the tee, three-putts the hole, and loses the playoff the following day. British golfers have avoided white tees ever since.

A superstitious player relies on luck, or some mysterious power, rather than his own skill. Don't make the same mistake. Purge yourself of all superstitions and depend instead on your abilities as golfer and golfman. But if you detect a superstition in your opponent, jump on it. For example, if you know he's partial to a certain brand of ball, be sure you play it too. Then you can casually "discover" the "coincidence" on the first tee, and magnanimously offer to play a different brand. The first time. The next time, well, fair's fair.

If your opponent exhibits an aversion to certain words or phrases (e.g., "out of bounds"), make him cringe by uttering them frequently. And just as it's considered bad luck to mention to a pitcher that he has a no-hitter going, so is it unseemly to point out that a golfer is working on a good round. Enough said?

THE LUCKY TEE Though it's a ridiculous notion that an ordinary wooden peg could improve one's game, that's exactly what you pretend. You tell your opponent you have a lucky tee, one you've been using for several rounds (never mind that the odds against not having broken or lost it are astronomical). Convince your opponent that you believe you're unbeatable when you use it, then put him on an emotional roller coaster. First "lose" it, giving him encouragement in spite of himself, then "find" it, making him feel doubly foolish: for buying into the superstition in the first place, and for actually being disappointed that you found your "lucky tee."

PURISTS

Sorry to say, there are golfers who would not let you play the game unless you do it their way. They're the high priests of golf fundamentalism, self-appointed keepers of the game, and they command you as follows:

I

Thou shalt not Mulligan, never, ever. Get to the course two hours early and hit balls to warm up. No exceptions.

II

Thou shalt call it a "flagstick," not a "pin"; a "bunker," not a "trap." Why? Because we said so.

III

Thou shalt not use titanium, or any other material more advanced than persimmon. (Purists are fixated on the technology that was state-of-the-art when they reached puberty.)

IV

Thou shalt not play "target golf." Young Tom Morris bounced it along the ground and by golly so shalt thou. No matter that most American courses are designed to make you fly the ball over hazards that don't exist in the British Isles. No, scrape the ball and take your medicine—for the good of the game!

V

Thou shalt not roll it over. "Winter rules" are never permissible, not even above the Arctic Circle.

VI

Thou shalt not care about thy score or thy handicap. Be *process* oriented, not *result* oriented. *Enjoy* the shanks, tops, and three-putts. Golf is *all* good.

VII

Thou shalt not care about winning. It is unseemly to actually *try* to win a golf match, and any such effort renders you a swine.

VIII

Thou shalt make a pilgrimage to Scotland, no matter how inconvenient, expensive, or crowded. No one may count himself a true golfer who has not tried to play the Old Course at St. Andrews in a howling gale.

IX

Thou shalt not ride. The golf cart is the Devil's own contraption. It prevents you from experiencing the game as it was intended. (Did even *Old* Tom Morris ride an E-Z-Go? We don't think so!)

X

Thou shalt not gamble on golf. The Royal and Ancient Game is too sacred to involve filthy lucre. (Unless you happen to run a big tournament.)

Defense: How to handle a purist? Be proof to his piety. Factor it into your course management the way you make allowances for a high wind or a hanging lie. Once you've done so, go on the attack:

Offense: Break the purist's commandments and defile golf's traditions at every turn. Hit out of order. Play an orange ball. Mispronounce golf terms and misquote golf clichés. Wear sandal-spikes. If all else fails against a purist: Did he know that A. W. Tillinghast was bisexual?

Note: If you, dear reader, count yourself a purist, please take no offense. You can still employ the purism gambit, albeit in reverse, and the execution is simple: Just be yourself.

During a practice round at Augusta National, Sam Snead finds himself one-down to young British Amateur champ Bobby Cole. As Cole is about to tee off on the 13th, Snead remarks, "You know, son, when I was your age, I used to hit it over those trees." Cole takes the bait and promptly drives into the pines, where it rattles around and falls into the creek.

"Of course," says Snead, "those trees were a hell of a lot shorter then."

Wonder to relate, golf is a game in which a forty-something can beat a twenty-something, in large part because the young tend to overestimate their abilities. For example, experts agree that most golfers use shafts too firm for their swing speeds, and young male golfers tend to take this to the extreme. They also have a penchant for low-percentage shots. And young men are a tad unsure of their masculinity. Thus if you discover that a young opponent uses regular shafts, you'll have a golden opportunity to impugn his virility by pointing out that his peers use extra-firm shafts.

Young golfers also tend to be preoccupied with equipment. They have inordinate faith in a new putter, driver, or multi-piece ball. But don't be intimidated the next time you're up against a young gun whose rig looks as though it belongs on the Tour. His equipment is probably better than he is.

I recently had the opportunity to "debrief" an age work victim. Playing a Southern California resort course with a young teaching professional, I managed to hit a solid three-wood off the 4th tee. When he acknowledged the shot, I replied, "Better than kissing!" (Actually, in keeping with the gambit involving the use of down-home-isms to annoy your opponent, I said, "Better 'n' kissin'!") After the round, the young pro admitted that though he knew "kissin' " was a euphemism, and he was sure I had been kidding, he still wondered, given my advanced age, whether there was some truth to the implication that hitting a golf ball replaces sex in later years. This he found to be a grim prospect, and he confessed to brooding on it for the remainder of the front nine, to the detriment of his game.

Of course, older golfers have their own vulnerabilities, not the least of which are chronic aches and pains and diminished strength and flexibility. The young golfman should try to understand that old age is not an identity but an affliction. The victim is seldom resigned to his fate, and most old people don't consider themselves "old." Exaggerated deference is thus surefire, especially when the age gap is under ten years. Pick up his tee for him, extract his ball from the cup, offer him a banana at the turn "for the potassium."

Low road: Send him a gift subscription to *Senior Golfer.*

EGO WORK

· · ·

Our antagonist is our helper. EDMUND BURKE

· · ·

"Just once, I wish I could play my usual game" is an all-too-common golfer's lament (and the inspiration for the title of a fine collection of golf essays by David Owen). The great Horace Hutchinson expressed it this way: "I do not remember having met any golfer who did not consider himself on the whole a remarkably unlucky one." And golf psychologists know that most players tend to regard their few good shots as typical, and all the others as aberrations. When they have a good round, they think, "If I can play this well now, I can play this well from now on."

Always strive to buttress these delusions in your opponent. Hence you're a wellspring of sympathy for his every misfortune, real and imagined. You console him for every fluff and foozle as if they were caused by the Devil himself ("Nice try!"; "Al*most!*"; "Well meant!") Reinforce his secret belief that his poor shots are anomalies, or the result of bad luck, or sudden wind changes, or "that damned *Poa annua!*"—the implication being that *Poa annua* is impossible to putt on and it isn't his fault he missed that eighteen-incher. That you are subject to the same conditions, i.e., you also putt on *Poa annua,* will never occur to him as he begins to feel even more sorry for himself. Commiserate for a string of "bad breaks." That drive he hit 240 down the middle of the 5th at Clown's Mouth during the drought of '93, *that* was the real him, and all the intervening slices, tops, whiffs, and shanks were flukes. We're cultivating a victim mentality here. (An easy task, golf being the most abusive game ever devised.)

You, on the other hand, should not kid yourself. Rather,

adopt the view of Walter Hagen, who said he *expected* to make six mistakes a round. When he hit a bad shot, he simply counted it as one of the half dozen and moved on. Let that be *your* standard. Anticipate setbacks, never allow them to discourage you, and do not worry about bad shots (though if Hagen expected six, you may have to allow for a few more).

Touring pros say the most common mistake of pro-am partners is not using enough club for a given shot. Indeed, most mid-to-high-handicappers are chronic underclubbers who'd sooner force a nine-iron than hit a smooth eight. Why? Because distance is so important to their egos, in effect they'd rather be short with a nine than on with an eight. That's okay—you'll be glad to accommodate them. When playing one of these gorillas, constantly reinforce his self-image. Tell him he's hitting it "longer than ever," and if he'd just caught a break or two, he wouldn't be four down.

A contrary yet equally effective ego gambit is never to acknowledge that your opponent is a long hitter. No doubt he's accustomed to such recognition, so lack of it will trouble him, and probably make him press for even more distance, which will ruin his timing and cause him to spray the ball. Or you might point to a spot twenty yards beyond his longest drive where you saw so-and-so drive it once. Your big-hitting opponent will probably come out of his shoes trying to reach it, and may even injure himself in the process.

FLATTERY WILL GET YOU EVERYWHERE

When your opponent is playing badly, compliment him on the one thing he seems to be doing right, and he'll probably stop doing it. Likewise, flattering him when he's playing well, though it may initially put him at ease, will soon make him examine his technique, and then try harder to justify your praise.

GUEST WORK

When your opponent is also your guest, you must first get beyond the canard that it would be impolite to beat him. Such misguided hospitality has no place in the repertoire of the true golfman. When you're the host, use your "home field advantage" to impair your opponent's game directly, through disinformation, and indirectly, by making him feel like an outsider.

Your guest-opponent will of course ask about local conditions such as targets on blind shots, hole locations, bailout areas, etc. In answering these queries, appear to be helpful while in fact misleading him. Never *lie*, just interpret, color, and "spin." For example, asked whether the 150-yard markers are accurate, say, "Yeah, right!" and chuckle. It will cast enough doubt to render them useless. If he presses the matter, be even more cryptic: "Well, it depends on which member of the greens committee you believe." This will conjure up whole worlds of intraclub conflict which, of course, have no place in the mind of a competitive golfer. And as the host, never miss an opportunity to provide fascinating details about local history and points of interest, native flora and fauna, and the course drainage system.

When you're the guest, you can neutralize your host's advantage by disparaging the design and condition of the golf course, the clubhouse architecture, the food in the grill, the selection of hair tonic in the locker room, etc. If you're a guest at a private club with strict rules of behavior (e.g., no cell phones, no shorts, no laughing), contrive a bizarre facial tic, or place a toothpick in the corner of your mouth and leave it there for the entire round.

SCARE TACTICS
Snakes

The most common form of snake work, of course, is to raise the prospect that your opponent may encounter a poisonous snake when he enters the woods or deep rough to look for his ball. That possibility, no matter how remote, will (1) limit the duration of his search, increasing the chances he'll have to declare a lost ball; (2) limit the scope of his search to the area immediately adjacent to the fairway, with the same result; and (3) make his swing even more tentative than usual if he does manage to find his ball.

But don't be too obvious. When your opponent is about to enter the rough to look for his ball, volunteer that you don't *think* it's snake season. Then cock your head and ask, "When *is* snake season, anyway?" If he asks what *kind* of snakes, inform him that rattlers are indigenous to most of the United States (some courses have warning signs you can point out to him). And by the way, did he know that recently killed rattlesnakes may bite—even with their heads chopped off? *Regional variants:* water moccasins, coral snakes, cottonmouths, copperheads, black mambas.

Lyme Disease

Once thought the basis of a strictly regional ploy, Lyme disease has obliged the golfman by spreading throughout the United States. Thus if you're playing "away" and your host-opponent is about to enter the rough to look for his ball, tell him to watch out for deer ticks. If he asserts that Lyme disease is unknown in the neighborhood, tell him you heard that a case has just been identified in the northern (or southern) part of the county. If you're the host, as your guest-opponent is about to enter the woods, tell him about poor old Fred, who contracted the disease *in the very same woods* and is now bedridden. Be sure to enumerate Fred's symptoms: the large red "bull's-eye rash," the aching joints, the chills and fever, the permanent neurological impairment, the cardiac arrest. If it's early in the season, say you read somewhere that experts are predicting a "banner year" for the disease. If it's late in the year, tell him that diseased ticks are especially voracious when the temperature drops.

Extra credit: Remind your opponent of Tim Simpson, who made the top-ten money list on the Tour in 1990, but whose career ended abruptly after he contracted Lyme disease in 1991. He suffered joint and muscle soreness and a severe case of the shakes, a permanent tremor in his left hand, and soon could not walk eighteen holes, let alone play competitively. He now works in auto racing.

Killer Bees

A similar approach can be used with "killer bees." The so-called Africanized honeybees have already arrived in the southwestern United States, and they continue to migrate northward. Point out that these angry insects are the most lethal species on their native continent, killing more people every year than poisonous snakes.

Nice touch: Remind him that Keith Fergus and his caddie were stung repeatedly by a swarm of *regular* bees at the '95 Nortel Open in Tucson.

Miscellaneous

Don't forget poison ivy, rabies—it's being found increasingly in bats and raccoons, especially in the eastern United States, *and there have been several deaths*—alligators, quicksand, and the hot dogs at the snack bar.

SOMETIMES A CIGAR ISN'T JUST A CIGAR

Though cigars have become fashionable in recent years with cigar dinners, cigar charity auctions, a cigar magazine, and a slew of celebrity endorsements, the cigar has long been a symbol of male exuberance. But for many, including a legion of feminists, cigar smoking is a filthy, antisocial habit, and a symbol of male arrogance. As a result of this backlash, cigar smoking has been banned at a growing list of venues, from office buildings to restaurants to clubhouses. But the golf course has traditionally been a safe haven for cigar smokers. Out in the open, away from women and children, a man can light up without fear of offending anyone. Sort of.

If your opponent smokes and you don't: Cite the medical evidence: Cigar smokers have a 34 percent higher death rate from various forms of cancer (lung, throat, larynx, mouth), and a significantly higher incidence of stroke, emphysema, and heart disease. And secondhand cigar smoke has ten times the carbon monoxide of passive cigarette smoke.

If your opponent uses a cigar tee, make fun of it. If he doesn't use one but merely places his cigar on the ground while making a stroke, ask him if he doesn't mind getting fecal matter on the tip (from the waste water used for course irrigation).

Advanced: Administer a dose of psychobabble by quoting Vance Packard: "The man who puffs on his cigar is sucking his thumb while the man who chews vigorously on his stogie is a nail biter."

If you smoke cigars and he doesn't: Insinuate he's a coward for not smoking and try to keep him downwind at all times.

If you both smoke cigars: Ask him why he removes the band. Or doesn't remove the band—there's confusion on this point: Whereas it used to be déclassé to leave the band on, it is now considered the mark of the connoisseur. Or vice versa.

If he smokes Cubans but you don't, impugn his patriotism. And by the way, has he heard about the counterfeit Montecristos (Partagas, Macanudos, La Coronas) flooding the country?

If you both smoke cigars but you smoke Cubans and he doesn't, be as condescending as possible. Pronounce it "Habana," and affect a wine vocabulary to describe yours: Draw deeply, exhale luxuriously, and sigh, "Ah, a distinct note of cinnamon, with just a hint of vanilla." He'll wonder why he only tastes smoldering cardboard.

YIPMANSHIP

. . .

The yips, it's the worst thing that can happen to you in golf. BYRON NELSON

The rot set in, so eyewitnesses have assured me, on the 71st green at Rochester in 1956, when he was well placed to win a record fifth U.S. Open. Not only did he miss the three-footer, which anyone could do, but he yipped it, and that was the beginning of the end. At any rate, my last memory of Hogan in competitive golf is at the Masters some years ago. Every green, as usual, is surrounded with spectators and, as the familiar white-capped figure steps through the ropes, everyone spontaneously rises to give him a standing ovation. And a moment later he is struck motionless over the ball, as though hypnotized, unable to move the ironmongery to and fro.

HENRY LONGHURST

. . .

Tommy Armour coined the term "yips" to describe the chronic putting malady that afflicted him in later life. He defined it as a "brain spasm which impairs the short game." By which he meant a nervous disorder in which the muscles jerk uncontrollably when the victim tries to putt or chip. The British call them "the twitches," and Henry Longhurst dubbed them "whiskey fingers" and likened them to trying to hit the ball with a live eel.

If anyone doubts their existence, in 1998 the Mayo Clinic launched a two-year study of the yips, the medical term for which is "focal dystonia." And a recent UCLA study found that the yips are related to advancing age, how long the victim has played golf, and "a tendency toward obsessional thinking."

· · ·

As I stood addressing the ball I would watch for my right hand to jump. At the end of two seconds I would not be looking at the ball at all. My gaze would have become riveted on my right hand. I simply could not resist the desire to see what it was going to do. Directly, as I felt that it was about to jump, I would snatch at the ball in a desperate effort to play the shot before the involuntary movement could take effect. Up would go my head and body with a start and off would go the ball, anywhere but on the proper line. HARRY VARDON

I have a classic case of the yips. You know, people say it's all in your head, but it's not a mental thing with me. I have a physical problem. When I sign my name, sometimes the pen jumps and there's nothing I can do. There's a loose wire back there or something. There's nothing you can do. JOHNNY MILLER

· · ·

Putative cures for the yips are numerous, diverse, and desperate. Sufferers try putting cross-handed, one-handed, or with the two hands wide apart. Some putt without looking at the hole, some look at the hole instead of the ball. Vardon, who called them the "jumps," tried putting in the dark. Some use a long putter, some a short one (Ken Green may hold the record at twenty-two inches—his toddler's). Bernhard Langer tried various unconventional putting styles, the most bizarre of which involved clasping both his right forearm and the putter shaft with his left hand. Langer also used a long putter, and eventually returned to a conventional style. Sam Snead employed a croquet stroke with some success until it was outlawed, then went sidesaddle. Gene Sarazen walked up and hit the ball all in one motion, fearing he would freeze if he took a conventional stance. Johnny Miller used what he calls the "I-don't-care" approach to fool himself into relaxing by pretending the putt was his second, or that he wasn't himself but rather one of his children facing the putt. "I call these W.O.O.D. strokes because they Work Only One Day," Miller says.

For your own peace of mind, knowing the real putting odds will help you avoid frustration, which in turn may help you avoid the yips. According to short-game expert Dave Pelz, touring pros—the best players in the world—miss half their six-footers and three-quarters of their ten-footers. When your putting expectations are unrealistically high, Pelz says, "you start worrying and blaming yourself, and that's where the yips start. Once the mind really believes you're going to screw up, it makes it happen."

If you discover that an opponent suffers from the yips, be sure to avoid doing or saying anything that might alleviate his distress. Then pick and choose from among the various gambits designed to capitalize on his misfortune.

For me, when facing a yippy opponent, the most effective ploy has always been to quote Ben Hogan, who said, after coming down with a severe case: "I get over the ball and I can't bring myself to bring the putter back. I say to myself, 'Hit it, Ben,' but the putter just won't move." This "giving sorrow words" approach, coupled with the implication that if Ben Hogan suffered from the yips, none of us mere mortals is safe, will allow your opponent to accept his lot and give up trying to overcome it. In this vein, you can "console" him with the knowledge that he's in "good company." Tell him that golf greats Bobby Jones, Gene Sarazen, Arnold Palmer, and Tom Watson all suffered from the yips. (*Caveat:* There's a contra view that acceptance may lead to relaxation, which may in turn cause abatement of the symptoms, but I'm aware of no empirical evidence to support it.)

Or take a page from Henry Longhurst who, when playing with a known yipper or shanker, would announce on the first tee: "I don't suffer from the shanks or the yips myself, but I seem to be a carrier." Then, at the turn, deliver the *coup de grâce* by quoting Longhurst again: "Once you've had 'em, you've got 'em."

Or take an even more direct tack. During a lull in the conversation, preferably before the round, blurt out to your opponent, "Ever get the yips?" Potter favors the straightforward, "Do you yip?" but betrays uncharacteristic ambivalence by calling it "one of the most questionable questions in Gamesmanship." Indeed, there are veteran gamesmen who insist that merely mentioning the yips is to golfmanship what nerve gas and biological agents are to warfare, i.e., that any civilized combatant would abjure their use. Which, of course, is bellywash. It is rank defeatism to forgo one of the most potent weapons in the golfman's arsenal.

BACKFIRE SYNDROME

Tom Watson and Jack Nicklaus are battling for the lead in the final round of the 1977 Masters, with Nicklaus playing in the group ahead of Watson. On the 13th, Nicklaus rolls in a birdie putt, extracts his ball from the hole, and then appears to wave it at Watson as if to say, "Take that!" Watson gets so angry, and so psyched up by Nicklaus's apparent gamesmanship, he makes a late charge to win the tournament. (He eventually confronts Nicklaus, who maintains he was only waving at the crowd.)

Just as there are people who seem to be immune to life's little annoyances, lucky folk who never seem to catch cold or get parking tickets, there are rare individuals who won't be fazed by the most potent gambits. They're simply impervious to gamesmanship. An even rarer breed: those for whom gamesmanship only acts as a stimulus. It actually motivates them to perform better. If you find yourself playing one, the only thing to do is cut your losses and avoid him in the future. But not to worry: It can be safely assumed under the laws of probability that any given opponent will not be one of these supermen, and that your gamesmanship will psych him out, not up.

PART IV

MATCHMANSHIP

MATCH PLAY BASICS

. . .

Match play has its own psychology, and it requires its own kind of cunning. The best match players have an ability to get inside the heads of their opponents and turn their weaknesses against them. In stroke play you play the course; in match play you play the guy walking beside you, and you play him not only with your golf clubs but also with your wits. DAVID OWEN

. . .

Medal play is checkers, match play is chess. In match play, the predominant form of competition for amateur golfers, you can play poorly and still win. A few match play fundamentals:

- Start slowly. Be cautious on the opening holes. Let your opponent's jitters and cold muscles get him in trouble.
- Always be aware of your opponent's situation and act accordingly. If he's in trouble, you play safe. If he's on the green in regulation, you go for it. When your ball is away and your opponent is in the rough, reconnoiter his position before playing your own shot. If his lie is bad, play more conservatively.
- Never concede a hole prematurely. Make your opponent earn everything he gets.
- It may seem obvious, but at match play, don't worry about your overall score. If you're concerned about

breaking 100, 90, 80, or 70 in addition to trying to beat your opponent, or if in the late holes you have a chance for a personal best or a milestone score, you'll put too much extra pressure on yourself. (Overall score often doesn't compute anyway because of the inevitable concessions in match play.)

By the time they reach the 17th tee in the final round of the 1972 British Open at Muirfield, Tony Jacklin and Lee Trevino are tied for the lead. Jacklin hits a good tee shot, but Trevino hooks his drive into a bunker, chips out, then hooks his third shot into heavy rough short of the green. Jacklin, meanwhile, has hit his second shot to within fifty yards of the hole. Whereupon Trevino surrenders. He congratulates Jacklin and cursorily hits his fourth shot over the green. Jacklin hits his third to within fifteen feet of the cup. Trevino, now just going through the motions, quickly jabs at his chip and . . . it rolls in the hole for a par! Which so unnerves Jacklin that he three-putts, giving Trevino the British Open.

Lesson: Never count your opponent out: There's nothing more demoralizing than watching the other guy pull off a miraculous shot to win a hole you thought you had in your pocket. A favorite Hagen gambit further illustrates the point: After driving into the woods, he would pretend to be stymied, pacing back and forth from the trees to the fairway, looking more and more troubled, and rendering his opponent increasingly sanguine about his chances of winning the hole. Where-upon Hagen would finally step up to the ball and hit a seem-ingly miraculous "recovery" shot stiff to the pin. Then he would grin and confess that the opening in the trees had been so big he "could have driven two Mack trucks through it."

TOURNAMENTS

Bobby Jones was right: There are two kinds of golf—golf and tournament golf. It's one thing to play your usual game on your home course, quite another to compete in the Crosby, or the Kip Addota Pro-Am, or even the Clown's Mouth Member-Guest. Here are a few keys to help you maximize your tourna-ment game and diminish your opponent's.

First, understand that *your team will not win*. No chance. There's a foursome in the field that will shoot net 52. Do grasp that. Second, know that *everyone* will be nervous. Normal first-tee jitters will be magnified a hundredfold. Which is why if you can swing smoothly and make solid contact with the ball, your aplomb will demoralize your opponents.

Pro-ams are the worst. You're playing with a professional, there are spectators, and it may even be televised (as in the case of the AT&T and the Bob Hope). Obviously, in these events the stakes are even higher. Not only do you risk humiliating yourself in front of a gallery, you're reaching a national audi-ence as well. Which calls for more extreme countermeasures. Consider James Garner's trick: Remembering that the focus will be on you and not on the flight of the ball, when you hit your shot, even if it's a snap hook or a cold top, hold your finish, smile, and stride briskly down the fairway. (Garner, a low-handicapper, admits to having done this on more than one occasion. The only time it failed, he confesses, was when his ball hit the camera lens.)

BETTING

· · ·

> Golf and wagering go together as smoothly as "double"
> and "bogey." JAMES Y. BARTLETT

· · ·

As Sam Snead remarked, there's nothing more boring than a walk in the park with three other guys. Which is why most players find that wagering enhances their enjoyment of the game. They may not be able to play particularly well, but they can still win a few bucks. It gives them *something* to be happy about. At least potentially.

But be clear: "Friendly wager" is an oxymoron. Never forget that *your opponent is trying to take your money,* and treat him accordingly.

If you're playing poorly in a Nassau, don't press. Pay your three-way debt (i.e., front, back, and match) and live to fight another day. On the other hand, if your opponent is having a bad round, allow him to keep pressing—the odds will be heavily in your favor. *Helpful hint:* Some golfers tend to forget lost bets, so to avoid arguments, write down all wagers on the back of a scorecard before teeing off.

When you beat someone with a lower handicap, never acknowledge—let alone apologize for—having received strokes. And never patronize him by saying he'll probably beat you the next time. He may think so, but he won't believe that you do.

GOLF HUSTLERS As for the blight on the game known as golf hustlers:

. . .

> One of these days in your travels, a guy is going to come up to you and show you a nice, brand-new deck of cards on which the seal is not yet broken, and this guy is going to offer to bet you that he can make the jack of spades jump out of the deck and squirt cider in your ear. But, son, do not bet this man, for as sure as you stand there, you are going to wind up with an earful of cider.
> DAMON RUNYON

. . .

Never bet anyone with his name stenciled on his bag. Never bet anyone who carries a one-iron. Never bet anyone with a deep tan but whose left hand is the color of mayonnaise. Never bet a guy named "Chick." Never bet anyone who's unemployed (too much time to practice). If a stranger offers you a stroke a hole, decline. If he's a right-hander and offers to play you left-handed, or vice versa, beg off. If he proposes a series of bets requiring audiovisual aids to explain, pass. And if a guy offers to play you with just a putter, or with a rake and a shovel, or a Dr. Pepper bottle taped to a stick, *do not bet this man*.

HANDICAPS

One of the great things about golf is the handicap system, which allows players of all abilities to compete on an equal—or, rather, equalized—footing. Theoretically.

According to the United States Golf Association, the average handicap index is 16.1 for men (and 28.9 for women). Which means the average American male golfer goes around the average par-72 course in about 90 strokes. But in my experience the average American male golfer seldom breaks 100. Why the discrepancy? Maybe my "anecdotal" evidence is unreliable. But then again, maybe the USGA's average handicap index is wrong. Maybe the average American male golfer's vanity causes him to deflate his handicap, either by posting fraudulently low scores, or by not reporting the high ones, or by playing fast and loose with the rules of golf.

In any case, if you're lucky enough to play someone whose ego is so out of control he fudges his handicap to make it *lower* (sometimes called a "reverse sandbagger"), try not to let your gratitude distract you. Play him as early and often as possible. If his car is in the shop, send a cab. Make sure he bundles up in cold weather. Is he getting enough fiber in his diet?

Conversely, the golf world is full of sandbagging swine who masquerade as higher handicaps than they are. (In polite circles it is said these handicaps "travel well.") You know the type: They always seem to win their Nassaus, and in tournaments, they win low net *and* low gross. How to handle a sandbagger? Insist on a match based on what you deem his true handicap or refuse to play him.

Lesson: Don't pad your handicap. Make sure it reflects your ability, no more, no less. Keep it accurate by playing the ball "down" and by putting everything out (i.e., by refusing gimmes, you'll learn to make short putts consistently and nullify the concede-early-don't-concede-late ploy). And when you have a bad hole, resist the temptation to give yourself a 7 instead of an 8. Otherwise, you'll have a built-in flaw in your competitive game, you won't be able to play to your handicap in matches where the rules are strictly enforced, and you'll be one of those pathetic creatures about whose handicap it can be said: "He can't *play* to it, but he can *pay* to it."

Maintain an accurate handicap, and you'll not only be *able* to play to it, you'll also be *confident* you can play to it. Which will give you a head start on the average American golfer.

PIGEON HUSBANDRY

The care and feeding of a bona fide pigeon—someone you beat regularly but who always comes back for more—is a delicate matter. You must strike a balance between winning consistently and still giving him hope of beating you. (I do not refer to this aspect of golfmanship as "hustling," which connotes smoke-filled pool rooms and other unsavory milieux. I prefer to think of it as "long-term planning.") The guiding principle is: Don't be greedy. Simulate vulnerability by, yes, allowing yourself to lose occasionally. When you win, attribute it to luck (your good, his bad). And never gloat over a victory. In short, always leave your vanquished opponent with the illusion of parity, and the hope of future triumphs. As said in another context: "Never drive your enemy to despair; it makes him strong."

SELECTION OF OPPONENTS Casting is crucial in movies and golf matches. If there's someone you know you can beat, by all means play him at every opportunity. But life does not always present us with tap-ins. It is sometimes necessary to go through a series of "auditions" to find the right person for the role of regular opponent. But be patient. The woods are full of bad golfers.

If you're responsible for awarding contracts or purchasing goods or services for your company, take advantage of "customer golf." A recent study confirmed what business people have always known: Salesmen don't mind losing if they think it will help make a sale. It's the way business has been done since time immemorial. If your opponent demonstrates such willingness, who are you to undermine Capitalism?

TEE TALK

. . .

More matches are lost through carelessness at the beginning than any other cause. HARRY VARDON

. . .

Mr. Vardon was speaking of slow starts, which he attributed to the failure to achieve the proper physical and mental state quickly enough. Indeed, how often have we seen it: three-over-fives after three, three-over-fives after nine! The same principle applies to first-tee negotiations:

Of course in every match your ultimate success will depend largely upon the terms on which you have arranged to play, before starting. The setting of these conditions is sometimes a nice matter, needing all the wisdom of the serpent in combination with the meekness of the dove. At such times you will be surprised to hear a person, whom previously you had believed to somewhat overrate his game, now speaking of it in terms of the greatest modesty. These preliminaries once arranged, however, you will find that he soon becomes himself again—till the next match-making begins.

HORACE HUTCHINSON

. . .

It's true: Golf matches are not won and lost on the fairways, nor even on the greens. They are won on the tee—the first tee—where the terms of play are negotiated.

That's why first-teemanship is so crucial. When you shake hands before the match, ask your opponent his handicap, and no matter what he answers, raise your eyebrows and say, "Oh, really?" Or, work into the conversation that you know someone who's "a nine *masquerading* as a twelve." If he's a sandbagger and has any conscience at all, the word "masquerading" will sting him. Or, plant a seed of doubt in his psyche while appearing to be assiduous about the rules: Walk up to him, extend your hand, and ask, "What brand is your provisional ball?" It's a perfect way to raise the specter that sometime during the round he'll hit out of bounds. Or, on the first tee, tell your opponent: "Sometimes I get so wrapped up in my game I may absent-mindedly step in your line or cough on your back-swing. If I do anything like that, I assure you it won't be intentional and I apologize in advance." Of course, you'll be in complete control of your actions throughout the round and will not commit any of these gaffes, but your opponent will nonetheless spend the first few holes dreading them.

FOUR PLAY

Most of the techniques in this book are designed for "average" opponents, i.e., people with "normal" sensibilities. But if you play in a raucous foursome in which there's a lot of razzing and wisecracking, profanity and flatulence, you'll have to up the gamesmanship ante just to rise above the background noise.

When traveling in one car as a foursome and your partner is the driver, seize the front passenger seat both coming and going. This breach of the unspoken rotation rule will create a tiny resentment that may well carry onto the course. "I'll show *him!*" your opponents in the back seat will mutter to themselves.

When playing in an arranged foursome, as when you have three and the starter assigns a single to your group, gang up on the outsider. Snicker at everything he says, ask rapid-fire, hostile questions, subject him to a barrage of inside jokes, running gags, and knowing glances at each other. In other words, pretend you're back in high school.

Conversely, when you're a single assigned to a threesome, divide and conquer. Identify the alpha dog and ally yourself with him. Try to detect latent animosities between them. Cast doubt on the number of strokes A gives B (privately tell A it's too many, B it's too few). Even intimate that one of them is cheating (through the use of pointed questions—avoid an accusation or you may have to back it up).

Regular groups have their inside jokes and pet phrases, and you can violate their privacy by appropriating them. For example, I was once grouped with three mortgage brokers from Plano, Texas, who played such a complex match—or rather, series of matches—it required two scorecards and frequent conferences to sort out their status. The core match was a skins game with the standard "one tie, all tie" provision. Whenever one made a putt to prevent another from winning a skin, the third man, who had been rescued, would shout, "Poosh!" Which I gathered meant "Push," i.e., the hole had been halved. The man who sank the putt would then echo it: "Poosh!" This idiotic ritual took me aback, but then I tried an experiment. What would happen if *I* yelled "Poosh!" at the appropriate moment? It didn't take long to find out. On the fourth green, broker A launched a forty-foot downhill-sidehill snake that hit the cup, bounced straight up, and fell in for a half. "Poosh!" I shouted. They all frowned. Broker C actually wrinkled a brow. They were clearly annoyed but didn't quite know why.

In a similar case playing with three strangers on a public course, one of them introduced himself as "Atkinson," but for

some reason his two cronies addressed him as "Ehtkeenson."
On the 12th green, I called him "Ehtkeenson" too. They *hated*
it. I had intruded on their inside joke. They all finished the
round in sullen silence and complained afterward about not
having played to their handicaps. Coincidence?

PARTNERSHIP

. . .

You must always, during the match, try to give your
partner in a foursome an impression that you are more
than pleased with him. This impression is usually a very
false one. HORACE HUTCHINSON

My partner always has a 1-iron in his bag; he has more
than 37 tags hanging from his bag; he has used the same
putter since he was five years old; he's gone if he tells
me about his marital problems on the practice tee.
GARY MCCORD

. . .

How to choose a partner? Generally, the best combinations
are a long-hitter and a short-hitter, a steady player and a
streaky one, a high-handicapper and a low-handicapper. In
any case, always maintain a united front. Never quarrel openly,
never needle or berate your partner, but never apologize to
him for a bad shot (Sam Snead always apologized once, on the
first tee, for any poor play to come). Keep your temper when
your partner loses his. Encourage him. Massage his ego. Coo
over his good shots and ignore his bad ones. And just as your

play should be complementary—known in golfing circles as "ham 'n' eggin' it" (i.e., when you have a bad hole, he has a good one, and vice versa), your golfmanship should ham 'n' egg it too. And never make a side bet with a partner: You don't want to be rooting against each other.

Nice touch: After winning a hole or getting a lucky break, call your partner "pardsie" within earshot of your opponents (similarly, "pard"; "pohdnuh").

When playing against partners, divide and conquer. Commiserate with A over B's mistakes by rolling your eyes in disgust as if to say, "What a shame you're saddled with this donkey." Insinuate to B that A can't play to his handicap. The implication, of course, is that they were beaten before the match began.

Caveat: Golfmanship is ultimately a solitary discipline, so partner golfmanship is tricky. Do not attempt it without careful planning and practice to insure that you and your partner are in sync.

SYMPATHY FOR THE DEVIL

It isn't easy to make an opponent feel sorry for you, which is why this should be classified as an advanced technique. Potter describes it as "game leg play," as in, "My leg is troubling me a little today." He designated its use in tennis as the Frith-Morteroy counter: "The pause, half-way through the second set, the grave smile, the reference to the 'ticker,' and the 'I'm supposed not to hit the ball too hard.'" Likewise in golf:

"Somebody pick that ball out [of the cup] for me. Suddenly, I can't stoop."

Thus you have an infirmity preventing you from playing your best, yet you're determined to *try,* earning both sympathy for your pain and admiration for your bravery. Examples:

- Slowly stoop to tee the ball, rising even more slowly, while simultaneously wincing and holding your breath (to make your face flush).
- Mention "that damned shrapnel," or the malaria you contracted in "'Nam" (the guilt evoked in a Baby Boomer who did not serve in Viet Nam can sometimes clinch an eighteen-hole match).
- Arrive at the course wearing a neck brace, then stow it in your bag before teeing off. If your opponent asks about it, mumble something like, "Oh, nothing, really, just a precaution."
- Pop a "pain pill" at the turn.

Caution: Be sure to carry the ruse through completely. Avoid abrupt or overathletic movements. If you affect a limp with the right leg, don't forget and start limping on the left.

BAD BACKS

. . .

I did go on the road with Ti[tanic Thompson], and there was one incident that made me realize that the man would stop at nothing to win a bet. We were in Ardmore, Oklahoma, mixed up in a tough nine-hole match against a couple of long hitters, $1,000 a man. We were dead-even going into the 7th hole, and I remember telling Ti we'd better shape up, the holes were running out.

"I know, I know," he said with a far-off look, like he was planning something. "Now you just go along with what I'm gonna do, and don't let it affect your game."

I had no idea what he had in mind, but then all of a sudden, he started staggering around like he was dizzy. Then he leaned down into the golf cart, put his head on the floor, stuck his feet straight up in the air, and started coughin' and wheezin'. Ti was about 75 years old at that time, he stood 6'4", and weighed maybe 145 lbs. soaking wet—he looked like walking death. He went through this routine for about five minutes and the other guys were major-league shook. They wanted to know if he wanted an ambulance, to go to the hospital, whatever.

"Oh no," he said, "Nooo. . . . I'd have to pay y'all. We got three holes to go and I'm damn sure gonna finish this match if it kills me."

Well now these guys are watching Ti's every move, afraid that he's about to croak on the course. Naturally, they start topping the ball, shanking shots—they could hardly concentrate at all. I could see that they didn't have a prayer, so I laid back a bit and beat them on the last hole with a par. LEON CRUMP

• • •

Back problems are a national epidemic, and they're partic-ularly common among golfers, whose spines are punished by the unnatural twisting of the swing. Bad backs have sidelined many of the game's greats, including Jack Nicklaus, Lee Trevino, Davis Love III, Fred Couples, Ernie Els, and Tiger Woods. Faced with such an injury, the only thing to do is follow doctor's orders, and get maximum golfmanship mileage from the disability.

Thus, hint that you have a problem early in the round, then soldier on bravely. Don't complain openly, just whimper when teeing up or marking your ball. If you're playing teams, have your partner tie your shoes and tee the ball for you. This will either shame your opponents into giving you more strokes, or at least make them feel guilty if they don't.

NO SYMPATHY FOR YOUR OPPONENT Obviously, you should express no sympathy for your opponent's infirmities. Nor for his tough luck: His fifty-footer lips out, his career drive lands in a divot, his approach hits a greenside sprinkler head and ricochets into the weeds; whatever the freak misfortune, under no circumstances should you acknowledge—let alone commiserate over—your opponent's bad breaks (other than in the execution of a specific ploy or gambit). Your stoicism will imply that his adversity is nothing remarkable, but merely part of the natural order, confirming his secret suspicion that the golf gods hate him.

THE ART OF THE GIMME
. . .

I don't fear death, but I sure don't like those three-footers for par. CHI CHI RODRIGUEZ

SYMPATHY FOR THE DEVIL:
Have your partner tie your shoes for you.

Putting affects the nerves more than anything. I would actually get nauseated over three-footers, and there were tournaments when I couldn't keep a meal down for four days. BYRON NELSON

· · ·

If the short putt isn't the toughest shot in golf, it causes the most anxiety, even for the best players in the world. Add a little golfmanship and short putts can be well nigh impossible.

The standard gimme ploy is to concede short putts to your opponent early in the round, then make him putt them down the stretch, so at a crucial stage late in the match he's suddenly faced with a tricky three-footer, and the sickening realization that he hasn't had to make one all day.

Walter Hagen put this gambit to lethal use against Joe Turnesa in the 1927 PGA Championship. Hagen conceded everything under three feet until the back nine, where Turnesa missed six short putts in a row to give Hagen the title. Gene Sarazen used it too, adding a bit of choreography: He would actually turn his back when an opponent had a short putt in the closing holes.

My position on the concede-early-don't-concede-late strategy is undecided. Though unquestionably popular, it may not be as useful as it seems. After all, a short putt is still a stroke, whether it comes early or late in the round. On the other hand, a miss may indeed be worth a lot more on the back nine, especially if there are presses in force. At any rate, when an opponent asks for a gimme and you decide to make him putt, your refusal should be polite but firm:

....

HIM: Is that good?
YOU: There's a lot of golf left in that one, by golly!

or

HIM: Is that good?
YOU (cheerfully): T'ain't bad!

....

On your part, never decline a proffered gimme, but never come out and ask for one. And by all means subtly encourage your opponent to give you short putts by deferring to him at every opportunity. Deference makes people generous.

On the 11th hole of the final in the 1998 World Match Play Championship between Mark O'Meara and Tiger Woods, O'Meara hits a nine-iron to within eighteen inches of the hole, Woods leaves himself a thirty-five-footer. O'Meara assumes Woods will give him the putt, but Tiger says nothing, so O'Meara marks his ball. Then Woods putts and misses, O'Meara concedes the next putt, expecting Woods to reciprocate, but Tiger says nothing. O'Meara thinks, "This is strange—he's going to make me putt it." He calls to Woods: "Are you crazy? You give me these at home!" Woods smiles, looks at O'Meara, and says, "Putt it!" He later explains: "What I wanted to happen, did. He started to worry a little bit about me instead of the putt. I started to get into his head. There was a little gamesmanship going on."

· · ·

Don't give anything and don't expect to be given anything. I've seen the best players in the world miss putts inside two feet, so no putt is a sure thing. If there's any kind of a sidehill or downhill contour, you'd be surprised how many "gimmes" can be missed. Certainly when you're playing for a lot of dough, you should hole everything. From four feet to two feet to one inch—putt it into the hole. It only takes a moment and it avoids all arguments. SAM SNEAD

· · ·

Always assume you'll have to putt everything out. When your opponent concedes a putt, pick up your ball immediately.

Do not putt it one-handed or halfheartedly as many people do (under the rules of golf, even if you do putt and miss, it's still good, but you don't want the anticlimax of putting and missing).

On rare occasions, giving a putt can actually be an offensive weapon:

On the last hole of the final match of the 1969 Ryder Cup, with the U.S. and British teams deadlocked, Jack Nicklaus concedes a two-footer to Tony Jacklin that halves the hole and the match. Nicklaus later explains that he didn't think Jacklin would have missed it, but he wasn't going to give him the chance. The gesture has been hailed as a shining example of sportsmanship, but what if it was a masterstroke of golfmanship? By giving Jacklin the putt, Nicklaus made the outcome technically an act of American benevolence, and cast eternal doubt on whether Jacklin would indeed have made the putt.

PART V

. . . . .

TRICKS
OF THE
TRADE

LAST-MINUTING

Walter Hagen was the undisputed master of last-minuting. He would saunter onto the first tee half an hour late for a match (when he knew he wouldn't be disqualified), or arrive within a minute or two of his tee time in a major championship. Which would invariably unnerve his opponents.

For avid golfers, a blown tee-time is a big disappointment. Hence the object of last-minuting: to create such anxiety in your opponent that he'll be late—to turn the screw on his nerves so tight—he'll be a basket case by the time he finally tees off.

When you meet your opponent at the course: Be as late as possible without losing your starting time. If you must arrive early to warm up, disappear before tee-off and reappear dangerously close to forfeiture.

When you pick up your opponent: Arrive on time but ask to "use the facilities," then sequester yourself for fifteen minutes (bring a paperback; reconcile your checkbook, etc.).

When your opponent picks you up: The courteous thing to do is to be waiting at the curb with your clubs, ready to go, especially if it's early in the morning. The courteous thing to do is to make things go as smoothly as possible. Therefore, invite him into the house, where you've spread the contents of your golf bag (balls, tees, windbreaker, sunscreen, Power Bars, etc.) in the hall. Try to be in the process of replacing your spikes when he arrives, and ask him to help (hand him the little wrench).

LAST-MINUTING: "That was *today?*"

When you're finally approaching his car with all your equipment, suddenly realize you've left something in the house, or announce that "nature calls" and retreat for twenty minutes (paperback, checkbook, etc.).

On the way: If you're playing your home course and your opponent picks you up, show him a "shortcut" that actually takes forty-five minutes longer. Other stress-producing passenger ploys include sympathetic braking, calling for a sudden turn, and the phantom engine noise (do not attempt unless you're an accomplished ventriloquist).

Advanced last-minuting: When your opponent comes to pick you up, answer the doorbell in your bathrobe, your hair tousled. Rub your eyes, squint at the morning light, and croak, "That was *today?*" (Extra points for wearing a nightcap.) Or, in perhaps the most outrageous—but proportionally rewarding—of all last-minute ploys, when your opponent arrives, invite him into the house, lead him to the kitchen, turn on your heels, and cry, "Who's for pancakes?" (Extra points for wearing an apron.) The prospect of cracking eggs and pouring circles of batter onto a griddle—let alone the melting butter and maple syrup—is worth two-up in match play and three strokes in medal. This is the proffer alone! If you actually *make* the pancakes, the potential is probably unlimited, but speculation will have to suffice because, as of this writing, the pancake ploy has never been taken that far. *Caveat:* For some reason, French toast isn't nearly as effective.

ETIQUETTE

Golf is an etiquette-intensive game, and any violation of its countless rituals and traditions is especially offensive, so you should know golf's conventions and observe them scrupulously. Unless ignoring them will afford some advantage over your opponent. Yes, for the golfman, etiquette is merely another instrument of conquest. Did I say "merely"? The premeditated faux pas is a potent weapon in your arsenal of annoyances.

Mock solicitousness is the standard etiquette ploy, excellent for the long haul. It is nicely illustrated by a scene in *School for Scoundrels,* a 1960 British film (Terry-Thomas, Alastair Sim) based on Stephen Potter's work. During a game of billiards, gamesman interrupts victim just as he is about to stroke a crucial shot, points to two old men quietly playing chess across the room and asks, "Are they bothering you?" Likewise you, trying to eliminate nonexistent distractions for your opponent. Which serves to (1) embarrass him and (2) break his concentration. Thus as he embarks on his preshot routine:

....

YOU: Are the carp bothering you?

HIM: Sorry?

YOU: In the pond at sixteen.

HIM: Why no, I . . .

YOU: They make an awful racket when they're feeding.

....

Similarly, does he mind the uneven ground in the tee box? Is your shadow in his way? On the green, what about the pine needles in his line? The possibilities are endless.

If your opponent is a known slicer and there's a group on the adjacent fairway to the right, though it may be a full fifty yards off his intended line of flight (the further the better), yell a preemptive "Fore right!" just as your opponent is about to begin his preshot routine. If he takes exception, look him in the eye and say, "Better safe than sorry," and remind him that etiquette is just consideration for others. Or cite a recent lawsuit in which a chronic slicer was held liable in damages for bodily injury because he failed to yell "Fore."

HONOR, SCHMONOR At top levels of competition, having the honor is considered an advantage on the assumption that a good player can gain a psychological edge with a good shot. Thus if A has the honor and hits a good drive, B will tend to press trying to outdo him. Now, a good player presumably has the confidence to *want* the honor, because he's reasonably certain to be able to take advantage of it. Not so for the average and below-average golfer, for whom having the honor can be a detriment if he leads off with a poor shot.

Therefore, "ready golf"—whoever's ready hits without regard to who won the previous hole—should be the standard for informal matches. It speeds play and, more important, enables the alert golfman to manage the flow of a match. Thus if you're swinging well and have your opponent on the ropes, seize the honor and close him out. But if there's trouble on a

given tee shot, or a strong wind, or a difficult clubbing deci-
sion, hang back and let your opponent blaze the trail.

Another simple but effective etiquette ploy involves calcu-
lated incivility. When your opponent considerately picks up
your wedge and hands it to you as you walk off the green, do
not thank him. It's an appalling breach of common courtesy.
Appalling.

RULESMANSHIP

Does everyone cheat? Probably not. Does everyone break
the rules? Of course. Golf is the most legalistic game ever
devised. *The Rules of Golf,* published by the United States Golf
Association in the form of a deceptively small booklet, is filled
with the kind of impenetrable legalese found in the Tax Code.
The USGA also publishes a separate volume, *Decisions on the
Rules of Golf,* 581 pages of "official rulings on over 1,000 golf
situations," (i.e., the "case law") including:

**1-4/3 Flagstick Stuck into Green Some Distance from
Hole by Practical Joker** [No relief.]

**1-4/8 Nearest Point of Relief from Cart Path Is in Casual
Water; Nearest Point of Relief from Casual Water Is
Back on Cart Path** [Better to concede the hole than try
to decipher this one.]

1-4/9 Bird's Nest Interfering with Stroke [Free drop.]

11-5/5 Ball Played from Teeing Ground of Hole to Be Played Later in Round Lifted; Ball Replaced at Spot from Which Lifted and Played Out When That Hole Subsequently Reached [Depends on definition of "stipulated round."]

13-2/37 Status of Moss or Creepers in Tree [Can't remove if on tree; can remove if on ground.]

14/4 Club Breaks During Downswing; Swing Stopped Short of Ball; Clubhead Falls and Moves Ball [No penalty if tee shot; one stroke penalty if ball was "in play."]

14/6 Ball Popped Up Swung At in Disgust [No penalty for "instinctive swing in anger."]

15/14 Ball in Bunker Deemed Unplayable, Dropped in Bunker and Played; Ball Then Discovered to Be Wrong Ball [No penalty.]

16-1a/11 Raised Tuft of Grass on Line of Putt Brushed to Determine Whether It Is Loose [If position of tuft is "altered slightly by the brushing" but has not become detached, no penalty—if player restores it to its original position before next stroke.]

16-1a/15 Mushroom Growing on Line of Putt [Discontinue play and request Committee to remove mushroom.]

18-1/7 Ball in Plastic Bag Moves When Bag Blown to New Position by Wind [Depends on definition of "outside agency."]

23/8 Worm Partially Underground on Line of Putt [No penalty for removal.]

23/10 Ball Embedded in Fruit [No relief.]

25-1b/25 Ball Enters Burrowing Animal Hole in Bunker and Comes to Rest Underneath Putting Green [See Rule 25-1b(i).]

On the pro tours, it helps if you're something of a "clubhouse lawyer":

In a Senior Tournament in 1998, the wind blows J. C. Snead's ball some fifteen feet away after he marks it but before he lifts it. He assumes he should put it back. He's wrong. The rule dictates that wherever the wind blows the ball, that's where you play it. If it blows it into a trap, you play it from the trap. If it blows it into the hole, you're deemed to have holed it.

Playing in the Masters, Jack Nicklaus's ball comes to rest on a peanut shell. He requests relief, but a rules official refuses to allow him to remove it on the ground that a peanut is a "natural impediment." Nicklaus, who religiously reads the rule book at the start of every season, isn't satisfied, and he comes up with an argument worthy of the Supreme Court. "It's a *roasted* peanut," he says, "so it's an *artificial* impediment." He wins his case and gets relief.

Unlike Nicklaus, most touring pros don't have a thorough grasp of the rules, which is why they consult a roving official before taking even the most obvious drop. It should thus come as no surprise that in match play, encyclopedic knowledge of the rules is a potent weapon in itself. Besides saving strokes, it can also prevent embarrassing blunders, especially when you combine your knowledge with healthy skepticism:

Playing an exhibition with Bobby Jones, Walter Hagen hits his ball into a trap, but Jones gets there first and throws a twenty-dollar bill onto the sand near the ball. Hagen promptly grabs it, and Jones even more promptly calls a penalty on him for picking up a "loose impediment."

On the 14th hole of the third round of the 1987 Andy Williams Open at Torrey Pines, Craig Stadler draws a muddy lie under a tree. To protect his trousers, he places a folded towel on the ground and kneels on it to hit the shot. After he completes his round, a rules official informs him that by using the towel to "illegally build a stance," he incurred a two-stroke penalty, and by failing to penalize himself the two strokes, he effectively signed an incorrect scorecard, an infraction punishable by disqualification. "I didn't read the decisions last year and I didn't read the rule book this year," Stadler explained. "One of these days I'm going to take a month off and read them both."

If necessary, you too should take a month off annually to read the rules and decisions, because if you're going to prevail against better players, you must know the rules intimately so you can mold them to your own purposes. Pay special attention to new rules. Keep a copy of the current edition of *The Rules of Golf* in your bag and don't be afraid to call an infraction against your opponent then and there, avoiding the common mistake of waiting until after the round to say something to the offender. (No matter what the outcome of the dispute, the prospect of another challenge is usually enough to deter intentional misconduct.) Cultivate a lawyerlike grasp of golf's legal intricacies so your pronouncements go unchallenged. The key here is to avoid the impulse to be "fair" or "consistent." An aspiring young golfman could do worse than to acquire his Juris Doctor—not with the intent of practicing law, I hasten to add, but to improve his rulesmanship.

THE SACRIFICE A disarming little rules gambit: On a hole you've already lost, call a penalty on yourself (e.g., for grounding your club in a hazard). Your apparent scrupulousness will confound your opponent, and make him think twice before accusing you of breaking a rule.

TEMPO WORK

"Tempo," the overall duration of the golf swing, is crucial in all phases of the game, from driving to putting. Many top players practice with a metronome to establish an even tempo, and Don January, the tall Texan with the languid swing and thirty PGA and Senior PGA Tour victories, advised doing everything slowly before a round, beginning with brushing your teeth.

Tempo is influenced by body chemistry, personality, and, most important, stress. The universal tendency is to get quicker under pressure. But to play well, your tempo must be smooth and deliberate, because a fast, jerky swing is almost always a bad swing. Thus if you can speed up your opponent's tempo, you'll go a long way toward beating him.

"Tempo" also refers to the overall pace of play—the rate at which a player walks the fairways, surveys the greens, etc.:

· · ·

Of course, there was gamesmanship out there [on the PGA Tour] that you had to deal with. But they were very natural about it. You take a look at who starts out walking real fast. Well, you know, good players like Mangrum, they're not going to change their timing. He'll slow down the fast walker, he'll walk twice as slow as he usually does. You see, a slow player is not only using his time, he's using your time. So you've got to go over and talk to him a little bit. JACK BURKE, JR.

. . .

All tempo work is based on the necessity that you, not he, shall dictate the pace of play. Behave opposite to your opponent and it will perturb his inner clock. If he's fast, you're slow, and vice versa (but remember that if you walk faster than usual, your own swing will tend to speed up too). If, on the other hand, he's rushing you, slow down. Pretend to agonize over club selection, check the wind by tossing pinches of grass in the air, re-tee the ball, repeat your preshot routine, take more time lining up putts, etc., etc., etc.

When it's your honor and your opponent tries to crowd you out of the tee box immediately after you've hit your drive, take even more time than usual to pick up your tee and vacate the area. Conversely, if he has the honor and hits a good shot, deny him the pleasure of admiring its flight by crowding *him* out of the tee box. But if he slices into the woods, give him lots of time to imprint the ugliness on his psyche.

If you're leading the match by a comfortable margin and hit into trouble, don't spend more than twenty or thirty seconds searching for your ball. On the other hand, if you're behind in the match, take the full five minutes, to break your opponent's momentum. If *his* ball is missing in action, make a big production of looking for it. It will add a measure of guilty discomfort to his regret over having hit an errant shot in the first place, and the longer you insist on looking, the more uncomfortable he will become.

Personal note: As a junior I got in the habit of using a moist towel to clean my clubs during a round (no doubt in imitation of tour caddies I'd seen on television). It is, after all, a useful practice. The cleaner the grooves on the clubface, the better the chance for a clean hit. But I'll admit it has become a ritual, and if I fail to clean the clubface after every shot, it makes me vaguely uncomfortable. I used to feel guilty about taking the time to do it, especially when using a cart (i.e., keeping my cart mate waiting while I rubbed), until I came to appreciate its efficacy. It seems that after you've hit your shot, your cart mate, whether driver or passenger, wants you to put the club in your bag and climb aboard without delay—he's eager to get to his own shot, after all. It's a matter of rhythm. But after a shot, most golfers take a moment at the bag to replace a head cover or to perform some other brief housekeeping task, so the man waiting in the cart will have subconsciously factored in the lag. That's why you must *really* scrub that club to lengthen the delay. (Examine the grooves from all angles, tilting the clubface to catch the light.)

Another wonderful way to break an opponent's rhythm is to spend a long time over a meaningless putt, or "accidentally" leave your pitching wedge on the previous green and have to go back for it. At the turn, a long phone call (to check on a hospitalized relative, say) will not only infuriate your opponent, it may also cause your group to lose its position on the tenth tee, a crushing blow to someone with "momentum."

SWINGUS INTERRUPTUS

There are few things in golf more upsetting than having your swing interrupted. But any such maneuver on your part carries the risk of branding you a blatant gamesman, so it should be used with extreme caution. Therefore, interrupt your opponent's swing only for a demonstrably legitimate purpose, as when there's an insect on his ball, or to remind him of his own swing thought.

WAGGLE WORK

. . .

Much dripping wears away a stone, and continual fussing and fretting . . . wears away the golfer.
BERNARD DARWIN

. . .

The waggle is an excellent way to begin the golf swing. This preliminary brandishing of the club at address breaks tension in the arms and wrists and promotes a smooth takeaway. As the old Scots used to say, "As ye waggle, so shall ye swing."

The waggle is not only important in diagnosing an opponent's nervousness, it can also be an offensive weapon. Once, after watching Hubert Green waggle seventy-five times in a sand trap, J. C. Snead said: "I promised myself that if he got to a hundred, I'd kill him." One is also reminded of Ed Norton's (Art Carney's) *Honeymooners* golf lesson in which his interminable waggling provokes Ralph Kramden's (Jackie Gleason's) mounting exasperation, which erupts when Norton finally demonstrates how to address the ball: "Hello, ball!"

Waggle work is indeed a great way to madden an opponent, but it involves a high risk of self-contamination, so don't try it unless you're sure you can handle it (as it were). On the other hand, if you're a fidgety person, you're a natural for waggle work and its allied gambits: repeated glances at the hole before stroking a putt, endless foot-shuffling at address (sometimes called "happy feet"), repetitive shirt-tugging, obsessive-compulsive ball-washing, etc. So, if you're the nervous type, give your jitters free reign. Let them express the real you, and unnerve your opponent.

THE MANGRUM

A simple but effective physical ploy named for its originator, the late Lloyd Mangrum, who would stand in his opponent's peripheral vision wearing white shoes and cross his legs as the man made his swing.

THE ROLLING START

A potent little gambit: On the tee, just as your opponent reaches the top of his backswing, start walking down the fairway. (To counter the rolling start, freeze at the top of your swing and shout, "One more player!")

1.

THE MANGRUM: 1. As your opponent addresses the ball, take a square stance, with 70 percent of your weight on your right foot. 2. As he begins his takeaway, your left foot releases. When he reaches the midpoint of his backswing, your left foot begins its looping move . . . 3. . . . . then accelerates to a strong finish. Think of the Mangrum as a mini golf swing. (Note: White shoes are best, but saddles will also work.)

2.

3.

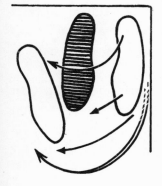

UPPER-RESPIRATORY WORK

Untimely coughing and throat-clearing are effective but controversial. They're among the most commonly used gambits, but purists insist they be confined to juniors. Perhaps they should be considered the training wheels of golfmanship, to be used temporarily by beginners while getting their balance.

Within this neanderthal genre, the "productive cough" is among the most difficult to execute. (If you must do cough work, for verisimilitude make sure you cough not only on your opponent's backswing but also at innocuous moments.) Similarly, the "hoccch," or "hock-a-looey," that grating throat-clear-cum-expectoration, should be approached with extreme caution. Shun it except in the most dire circumstances, as it carries the risk of involuntary hospitalization if your opponent happens to be a physician.

Whereas the cough or throat-clear is likely to be seen as rudeness or as an aggressive act of gamesmanship, a sneeze is involuntary, and for me the only worthy upper-respiratory ploy. But make sure it doesn't degenerate into cartoonish bad acting. (It helps if you're known to suffer from hay fever.)

THE STIFLED SNEEZE A *stifled* sneeze is much easier to simulate: You turn away abruptly, put your hand to your mouth, inhale audibly, and say, "Tchtt!" You will get credit for trying not to disturb your opponent, all the while making more of a commotion than if you had simply sneezed normally. (Requires practice.)

THE STIFLED SNEEZE: Coordinate the movements of the stifled sneeze with your opponent's swing: 1. As he waggles, your nose wiggles. 2. As he takes the club back, you begin inhaling while simultaneously lifting your chin in the classic pre-sneeze "load-up." When he reaches the top of his backswing, so you have reached the "top" of your inhalation. (Note that head position is just short of horizontal.) 3. As he begins his downswing, you "pull the trigger": Lurch forward, downward, and to the side, while keeping the lower body "quiet."

Note: an otherwise involuntary upper-respiratory function has been taken to new heights by a 22-handicapper from Chicago who shall remain anonymous. An asthmatic, he is able to wheeze at will, to his inestimable advantage from tee to green.

A NOTE ON RUDE NOISES

· · ·

Few pleasures on earth match the feeling that comes from making a loud bodily-function noise just as a guy is about to putt. DAVE BARRY

· · ·

Dave Barry is a terrific writer and a very funny guy, but he would flunk Golfmanship 101. Making loud bodily-function noise ranks with Velcro-ripping as the most adolescent of tactics, pathetic attempts to compensate for lack of talent. Just as brute force is amateurish and self-defeating in the golf swing, so too is such crudeness in the execution of golfmanship. Unless you can vomit on demand.

GREEN PLAY

The short game is to golf what the end game is to chess: delicate and crucial. Putting and chipping account for at least half the average player's strokes, so golfmanship applied on and around the green has a heightened effect on the outcome of a match:

Lew Worsham turns the tables on master gamesman Sam Snead on the 18th green of the 1947 U.S. Open playoff at the St. Louis Country Club. The two are all square. Worsham, who faces an easier, uphill putt, wants to hole out first to increase the pressure, so he interrupts Snead just as he's about to stroke his three-footer. "Wait a minute," says Worsham. "Are you sure you're away?" A measurement indicates Snead's ball thirty and one-half inches from the cup, and Worsham's an inch closer. Snead tries to regroup, but he misses the putt. Worsham makes his to win the championship by a stroke.

LINE-STEPPING Line-stepping is a provocative and, some might say, boorish tactic. If you choose to step in your opponent's line, do it once, early in the round, and make a big show of apologizing. Then, on subsequent greens, come perilously close to doing it again. Your opponent will never quite relax. Again, it's aggressive—and I don't argue with those who find it downright tacky. Nor do I argue with those who find it downright effective.

Though it's a flagrant breach of etiquette to walk in an opponent's line, there's no stigma to crossing in front of an opponent—i.e., between him and his ball—while he's trying to line up his putt (ideally, just as he has begun to plumb-bob). It's much more elegant than stepping in his line. As is standing in the *slightly* wrong place while he's lining up, and then being solicitous about moving away.

PLUMB-BOBBING Plumb-bobbing is a controversial method of lining up putts. You hold the butt of the putter between the fingers and let the head hang free like a lead weight at the end of a string. Then you close one eye (with your "dominant eye" open) and sight the hole, keeping the ball aligned with the vertical shaft. The relation between the hole, the ball, and the shaft supposedly reveals the break. If the ball and shaft are to the right of the hole, the putt will break left, and vice versa.

In a recent informal survey, eight out of ten players who use this method could not articulate why it works, and six out of ten could not even explain *how* it works. They just go through the motions of plumb-bobbing as if it were some voodoo ritual, then read the putt in the conventional manner.

Therefore, when pitted against a plumb-bobber, at a crucial stage in the match, as he raises the putter to sight the line, smile innocently and ask, "Why do you do that?"

Conversely, if you're a plumb-bobber, do it proudly and defiantly. It's mysterious, and will thus intimidate non-plumb-bobbers. If your opponent questions you about it, tell him it improved your putting "a thousand percent" and ask him if he would like to learn how to do it. After the round.

POSITIONING Stand across the green in your opponent's line of sight and practice your stroke. If he asks you to move, say, "Oh, gee, sorry" and move away quickly. Extra credit for little tiptoe steps.

SHADOW WORK If your opponent asks you to move your shadow, comply immediately. But don't move it *enough*. Then he will either (1) have to ask you again, or (2) proceed with the shot under duress. Either way, you've upset him. Conversely, when your opponent's shadow disturbs you, do not mince words: Look right at him, frown, and bark, "Shadow!" This will startle and embarrass him. He may even pull a muscle jumping out of the way.

BALL-MARKING When your ball is directly in your opponent's line, mark it quickly and tamp down the coin or plastic marker with your putter. Hard. That way, if your opponent asks you to move the marker further out of his line, there may still be an indentation that might cause his ball to bounce off line.

But consider putting out rather than marking. Good players like to get in the hole first to put added pressure on their opponents. And putting first has an additional advantage: You don't have time to think about ways to miss. So, instead of marking after a lag putt, go ahead and knock it in. You'll have less time to choke.

In the 1996 Senior U.S. Open, Tom Weiskopf complains that his playing partner, the reigning U.S. Senior Amateur Champion Jim Stahl, marks his ball with a quarter. Weiskopf is quoted as saying, "Ask anyone who has ever played golf. When you are three feet or less from the hole near someone's line, you don't mark the ball with a quarter. You mark it with a nonreflective penny." Stahl is dev-astated: "I'm crushed about this whole thing," he says after missing the cut with a pair of 80s. "I've never been treated like this in my life."

Tom Weiskopf's protocol notwithstanding, the rules re-quire only that you mark your ball so you can return it to the same place, and you may use anything reasonably designed to accomplish that. So, for the golfman intent on distracting an opponent, originality counts. Use a distinctive foreign coin, say, or a driving-range token (better yet, a subway token). Or an antique button. Anything that might seem vaguely inap-propriate. One golfman I know uses a polished Mercury dime. He says it's inconspicuous and usually goes unnoticed for an entire round, but if his opponent is of a certain age and does happen to recognize it, it never fails to generate a wave of nos-talgia that tends to drown out other things—like putting.

DISINFORMATION When you leave your forty-footer ten feet short and your opponent has yet to putt, it's a perfect opportunity to mislead him on the speed of the green, but be advised: Misinforming your opponent about playing condi-tions is a delicate matter. You have to be careful not to break the rule that prohibits giving advice. But if you and your opponent are on the same line and you're away, and you hap-pen to leave your putt short, you may be able to salvage the hole by saying to yourself in a stage whisper, "Really *belted* it, too."

FLAGSTICK WORK When your ball is on the putting surface, you will be penalized two strokes in medal play or loss of the hole in match play if your putt strikes the flagstick. Which of course is why the pin must either be tended or removed. Which in turn presents opportunities for the alert golfman.

For example, experienced caddies never bend the flagstick when tending it—it makes it hard to extract it from the cup when the ball approaches. Thus when tending for your opponent, *bend the pin*. The mere sight of it bowed will probably unsettle him. And he will have to either ask you to unbend it (and sound like a prig) or try to ignore it and putt under a cloud. When you pull the pin for your opponent, dropping it on the green (slap!) at a crucial stage in his takeaway is crude, but dropping it during his setup is less blatant but still effective. On windy days, a good caddie will gather the flag and hold it against the pin to keep it from flapping loudly. Need I say more?

SPIKING Raymond Floyd once complained that green play was rampant when he joined the Tour in the early sixties: "The older guys would try to intimidate younger players. Veterans would walk or move a little bit just as you were about to play. You had to say something to them or it wouldn't stop. I did." Established players would purposely leave "tracks": "They'd deliberately spike up the greens," Floyd said. "It was unbelievable how high those spike marks would be around the hole! You'd get up to a putt and have just about no idea where

THE BALL-BOUNCE: 1. Use a high-lofted club to scoop the ball off a grassy lie, then bounce it on the clubface. Keep your eye on the ball, not the club. 2. Do a quick right-face, launch the ball into a high arc, and catch it in the palm of your left hand.

the ball would end up." Unfortunately, whether deliberate spiking of the putting surface is legitimate need not concern us because, with the advent of Softspikes, it's a lost art.

THE BALL-BOUNCE

Bouncing a ball on the face of an iron and then flipping it into your hand is one of golf's most impressive parlor tricks. It's difficult to master, and you'll never see a high-handicapper doing it (it's a skill acquired on the practice range, after all) so your time working on this technique will go further to intimidate opponents than hours of practicing ordinary shots.

PART VI

. . . . .

CONVERSATION: THE FIFTEENTH CLUB

CHATTER

. . .

No golfer can really play to the utmost of his game who is discussing politics, the crops, the weather, and the grouse. HORACE HUTCHINSON

If conversation was fertilizer, Trevino would be up to his neck in grass all the time. LARRY ZIEGLER

I'm very tightly wound. All that jabbering is a pressure valve. I couldn't do without it. LEE TREVINO

. . .

Lee Trevino is the undisputed champion talker of professional golf. Using badinage to addle opponents is as much a part of his game as his trademark looping backswing. When Tony Jacklin once said to him on the first tee, "Lee, let's not have any conversation today," Trevino replied, "Tony, you don't have to talk, you just have to listen." Gary Player has perhaps the best defense: "If you walk behind him, you can get some serenity," he says. Most of Trevino's competitors on the Senior PGA Tour are resigned to his motor mouth, but Raymond Floyd, for one, is not amused: "There are some guys who get away with a lot because they make people laugh. They throw the barbs and needle a guy all day, and then they just pass it off by saying, 'It was all in fun.' But it isn't always fun to be on the receiving end." (Trevino isn't sociable *off* the course: "I've had dinner with three players in fourteen years out here. I don't want to get to know these guys. With nine holes to play, I want them to worry about not knowing me," he says.)

Lee Trevino's constant chatter is effective because, sooner or later, he's bound to hit on *something* that will upset his opponent. But Trevino is a natural talker, and his palaver relaxes him. If that suits you, fine, but make sure you can bring it off before you employ conversation as a weapon. (Conversely, should you find yourself playing a Trevino type, stay as far away from him as possible by taking separate carts, separate routes to the green, etc. Try to keep out of earshot between holes. Do not laugh at his jokes. Keep a pair of ear plugs in your bag and slip them in when the blather gets unbearable. And keep pre- and *après*-golf fraternizing to a minimum, because the more contact, the more conversation, and the more conversation, the more contamination.)

One conversational gambit is practicable for most of us: Affect a bad foreign accent. When your opponent stripes a drive down the middle, or sticks an iron close to the flagstick, exclaim, "Auch, that's a fine golf shot, laddie!" When he yanks his tee shot into the rough, shake your head and say, "*That*'ll be buried in the bracken!" When it starts to rain, quote the Scottish proverb: "If it's nae rain and it's nae wind, it's nae golf." If you can't manage the accent, employ such basic Scottishisms as "wee ball" and "laddie-buck." The pretentiousness will drive your opponent up the wall. If he happens to be of Scottish or Irish ancestry, go British: "Beastly luck!"; "Well judged!"; "That's a job done nicely!"

But if you really want to exasperate, try some of that grating, down-home slang favored by Dan Rather: "That old dog won't hunt!" (anemic approach putt, ninety-yard drive, etc.); "You're livin' on the lucky side of the road!" (his ball bounces on a cart path and ends up in good shape); "That's enough to make a Texas preacher lay his Bible down!" (faux commiseration for your opponent's "bad luck"); and the all-purpose exclamations, "Don't that beat a hen a-flyin'!" and "Don't that take the whole biscuit!"

At bottom, conversational gambits epitomize one of the basic principles of golfmanship: Keep your opponent mired in irrelevancies.

GIVE 'EM SOMETHING TO THINK ABOUT
· · ·

> It is not altogether to your advantage while standing over a 5-iron shot to be thinking, "I've got to remember to get some Freon in the Toyota." DAN JENKINS

· · ·

The kind of concentration necessary for championship golf is exemplified by the British women's amateur champion Joyce Wethered, who, when asked if the thundering of an express train a few dozen yards away had disturbed her putting, replied, "What train?"; by José-María Olazábal, who said of a streaker at the British Open, "It was only a naked woman"; and by Jack Nicklaus's famous statement, "I couldn't care less who I'm paired with." Chances are, your opponent will not be a Wethered, an Olazábal, or a Nicklaus, and *his* (her!) concentration will be astonishingly easy to break by simply complimenting him on it. But in the unlikely event you do find yourself struggling against someone with acute concentration, stronger medicine may be necessary:

· · ·

How many people realize that every part of the swing is associated with irrelevant and putting-off thoughts? It is these irrelevant thoughts, always latent, which the gamesman must try to bring to the surface, however buried and fleeting they may be. STEPHEN POTTER

· · ·

Walter Hagen was a genius at planting "putting-off thoughts" in an opponent's mind. For example, whenever he found himself losing to a young player, Hagen would cajole him with false friendliness. "After you win this tournament, we'll go on tour together," he would promise. The young man's head would swim with visions of fame and fortune, his concentration would disintegrate, and Hagen would win the match. And never mention the "tour" again.

The annals of golfmanship are replete with other examples of the disastrous effects of extraneous thoughts:

Harry Vardon, six-time British Open champion and inventor of the overlapping grip, misses a three-foot putt to tie Ted Ray for the 1920 U.S. Open championship at Inverness. A man in the gallery asks Vardon how a great player could miss such a short putt, and Vardon decides to give him an object lesson. He bets the man a hundred dollars he can't make the same putt, even if he practices for an entire week. A week later a big crowd gathers to watch, and of course he misses the putt. He's had seven days to think about it.

Just before the playoff between Arnold Palmer and Jack Nicklaus at the 1962 U.S. Open at Oakmont, Palmer asks Nicklaus, "Do you want to split the money?" The twenty-two-year-old Nicklaus, in his first year on the Tour, is taken aback. He doesn't know purse-splitting is a common practice among professionals. He politely declines the offer and shoots 71 to Palmer's 74 to win his first U.S. Open. Looking back, Nicklaus characterizes Palmer's offer as a "nice gesture." But the trained games-man will interpret Palmer's intent only one way: He wanted to give the rookie something to think about.

Tom Watson and Ian Baker-Finch share the lead after three rounds in the 1984 British Open at St. Andrews. Just before teeing off on Sunday morning, Watson leans over to the twenty-three-year-old Baker-Finch and says, "This is the first tee of the last round of the British Open. If you're not nervous, you're not human." Baker-Finch promptly dumps his approach into the Swilcan Burn and goes on to card a 7-over-par 79 to lose the championship to Watson.

An unknown club pro from North Carolina named Roland Hancock reaches the final two holes of the 1928

U.S. Open at Olympia Fields with a seemingly in-surmountable lead. As he walks onto the 17th tee, a spectator shouts, "Make way for the next U.S. Open champion!" Hancock promptly double-bogeys the 17th and 18th, missing a playoff by one stroke.

Dai Rees is playing the final round of the 1946 British Open at St. Andrews after tying Sam Snead and Johnny Bulla for the 54-hole lead. On the 5th tee, a friend approaches Rees and says, "For heaven's sake keep your head. Everyone is playing so poorly, you'll win if you just play your game." Rees's game immediately deserts him and he finishes with an 80, losing to Snead by five strokes.

Ken Venturi has a four-stroke lead in the 1956 Masters. As he walks onto the first tee for the final round, a friend tells him: "You're going to win! You're going to be a mil-lionaire!" Venturi, thinking about money instead of golf, shoots 80 and loses the championship.

In the 1993 Ryder Cup at the Belfry in Sutton Coldfield, England, Davis Love III and Constantino Rocca are fighting a close match until the 17th green, where Rocca has a three-footer to stay one-up going to the final hole. But Rocca lips it out—and walks dejectedly to the 18th tee. Love begins to follow him, until the U.S. captain, Tom Watson, tells Love to stay on the 17th green and hit a few practice putts—to give Rocca extra time alone to think about the disaster. Love wins the final hole and the match.

The practice of "icing the kicker" or the shooter is based on the same principle: Facing a crucial field goal attempt or a clutch foul shot against him, a coach calls a time-out to give the kicker or shooter more time to think about his task. Likewise, the longer you can make your opponent wait before playing a crucial shot, the harder it will become:

· · ·

Jenny [Chuasiriporn] should have won [the 1998 U.S. Women's Open]. Se Ri Pak iced her big-time on the last hole when she hit her ball into the water hazard. It took Se Ri a good twenty minutes to hit that shot from the hazard, which to me is a blatant violation of the rules of golf. Jenny stood out there in the fairway and totally lost her rhythm while Se Ri was busy unduly delaying play. The importance of what was about to happen finally dawned on Chuasiriporn, and she turned an easy par into a heartbreaking bogey. JOHNNY MILLER

· · ·

When Colin Montgomerie reaches the 71st green at the 1997 U.S. Open at Congressional, he shares the lead with Ernie Els and has a five-footer for a scrambling par. Instead of knocking it in and moving on, he waits in a huff for the commotion behind the nearby 18th green to die down. After several minutes of fuming, he finally hits the putt, and misses, eliminating any chance to win. Here, in a rare case of unintentionally self-directed gamesmanship, Colin Montgomerie ices himself!

Nothing is more irritating than a self-congratulator, so praising your own game will almost certainly distract your opponent. When you spank a tee shot two hundred yards or hit a wedge to within twenty feet of the hole, puff up your chest and exclaim, "I'm da *man!*" Your opponent will think you're a self-satisfied boor, but he'll be thinking you're a self-satisfied boor instead of about his game. Or you may want to do a victory jig (à la those colorful NFL end-zone dances) when you sink a long putt (or a short putt, for that matter) or hit a long drive (or a short drive). Nothing elaborate—just a few simple steps (be sure to rehearse). Other annoying self-celebratory gestures include the standard arm pump, the Tiger Woods arm pump (not recommended for seniors), and the in-your-face exclamation, "Yes!"

Nice touch: Tip your hat to an imaginary gallery.

Advanced: Rip off your shirt to reveal a black sports bra and take a victory lap around the green or tee box.

JAPANESE ADMIRALS In the Introduction to the 1993 edition of his golf memoir *The Bogey Man,* George Plimpton warns readers about the first chapter, wherein he writes of "Japanese admirals," an image that intrudes on his consciousness when he addresses the ball. He reports that since publication of the first edition in 1967, some readers complained that they too had begun to suffer from the Japanese admirals, so he advises readers of the present edition "who own delicate games just barely on the edge of chaos and for whom mental equanimity is essential" to *skip the first chapter*. Therefore, a copy of the 1967 edition (available from used booksellers) would make a perfect gift for your opponent.

There's a whole species of "putting-off thoughts" involving off-course activities:

. . .

Back in 1955, in Detroit at the P.G.A. National, I was due to play Snead in the afternoon. Al Watrous had defaulted to me and Sam had to play somebody else that morning. It was an easy match for him, so he just knocked his opponent off real fast and was walking into the clubhouse as I was coming out. This was at the Meadowbrook Country Club and Chick Harbert was taking air reservations back in the clubhouse for the guys who thought they might be beaten in the afternoon round.

So, when I bumped into Snead, I said: "Sam, Chick is taking reservations back there; where are you going—to White Sulphur Springs or Boca Raton?" Without thinking, Sam said: "Why, I'm going home to White Sulphur," and, believe it or not, he went in there and made reservations. I know it for a fact because Chick told me so. It evidently didn't strike him until he had made the reservation and when he came out and met me on the practice tee, he grinned and said: "Well, I made reservations for you too."

That's all there was to it, but it was just enough to throw him off and he was easy as pie. Three and two I beat him and when he left the sixteenth green he never even started to the clubhouse, he just went straight to the parking lot. People trying to stop him for his autograph, practically got walked over. Sam was sore and I don't blame him. He was sore at himself for letting me get to him, and match play is full of that kind of stuff.

TOMMY BOLT

. . .

Are there arrangements *your* opponent must make that can't wait until after the round?

. . .

Perhaps the most fatal beam of all that can float over your mental vision is the vision of a past hole played badly which you are filled with some insane notion of "making up for." The idea of "making up," by present extra exertions, for past deficiencies is one of the most deadly and besetting delusions that is prone to affect the golfing mind. Its results are *inevitably* ruinous.

HORACE HUTCHINSON

. . .

When your opponent suffers a disaster, put your arm across his shoulder and whisper in his ear, "That's okay, *you'll make up for it* on the next hole."

Another benefit of giving your opponent something to think about is the dawning awareness that he's being games-manned. This will make him determined to outthink you, which will almost certainly cause him to outthink himself.

SWING THOUGHTS

. . .

Too much thought about the mechanics is a bad thing for anyone's game. . . . You must be mindful but not thoughtful as you swing. You must not think or reflect; you must feel what you have to do. PERCY BOOMER

One thing you don't ever do is think of bad things when you're over a ball. FRED COUPLES

. . .

"Swing thought" is a contradiction in terms, because when you *think* about the golf swing in all its complexity, you cannot execute it properly. The goal is to think of nothing, to banish all conscious thought and trust your muscle memory. For most of us, that's easier said than done. We're at the mercy of countless distractions, both real and imagined, from buzzing insects to our own stream of consciousness.

Even top professionals have these problems, and many of them find it helpful to focus on a predetermined sound or word at address. Some suggest the sound of a dial tone. Tom Watson recommends the word "Edelweiss": "Think 'E . . .' on the way back, 'del . . .' to the top, and 'weiss' coming down." Johnny Miller uses a two-word, two-syllable name: Take the club back on "Cin-dy," and through the ball on "Craw-ford."

But a "swing thought" is something else, a last-second reminder to avoid a flaw or bad tendency you've worked to correct on the practice tee. For example, Davis Love III has three swing thoughts:

1. Have a gameplan.
2. Pick a specific target.
3. Slow off the ball.

Likewise John Cook:

1. Keep chin up.
2. Turn toe open away from ball.
3. Keep knees flexed through impact.

And Annika Sorenstam:

1. Pick your target and trust your aim.
2. Maintain a smooth tempo throughout your swing.
3. Commit 100 percent to the shot and don't worry too much about the result.

Pat Bradley has four:

1. Extension.
2. Extension.
3. Extension.
4. Extension!!

As does Jim Furyk:

1. Square clubface at address.
2. Consistent ball position.

3. Relax forearms and hands.
4. Good rhythm and tempo.

Well and good for the pros, but as Bobby Jones noted, the average amateur swings best when he has the fewest things to think about. Mickey Mantle had the same idea: "I never think about anything during the [golf] swing. I just hit it. The same thing with batting. Once you're in the box, it's too late."

Which is why the simple question "What's your swing thought?" is so effective. If your opponent doesn't have a swing thought, he'll wonder if he should get one. If he does have a swing thought, he'll question its effectiveness.

BALL WORK

Recent advances in golf ball technology, the proliferation of new brands and subbrands—and all the attendant confusion—provide fertile ground for the golfman. Any mention of a fabulous new ball (and there always seems to be one or two on the market) will undermine your opponent's confidence in his own ball.

When your opponent puts a fresh ball in play, tell him about Ben Hogan's strange routine. According to biographer Curt Sampson, Hogan always used six balls per round, a new one on each of the first three tees. Then he used the first ball on the 4th tee, the second on the 5th, and so on. On the back nine, he repeated the procedure, using a new ball on the 10th, 11th, and 12th tees, etc. Why Hogan did it precisely this way is not explained. *Perhaps your opponent can come up with an answer.*

Hogan tested new balls by floating them in bath water and Epsom salts and spinning them to check symmetry. If one side floated downward, he knew the internal rubber bands had been wound unevenly and the ball was lopsided. He was also known to have rejected new balls because of minute paint imperfections. Golf balls are no longer "painted" per se—the pigment is chemically bonded to the cover—nor are most of them filled with rubber bands. But after you describe Hogan's testing procedure to your opponent, casually inquire if he's heard the rumors about poor quality control at Spalding (or Dunlop, or Titleist, depending on the ball he plays).

If you notice your opponent licking his ball to clean it, cite the documented case of the sixty-five-year-old Irish golfer who contracted hepatitis as a result of doing so. "Golf ball liver," they call it. Be sure to enumerate the symptoms: fatigue, depression, stomach pain, jaundice. Explain that it's the *Agent Orange* they put on the greens that causes the liver damage, and that *the toxic effect is cumulative.* A confirmed ball-licker will dwell on this information for the rest of the round, perhaps for the rest of his life.

SARCASM

. . .

Of all the griefs that harass the distress'd,
Sure the most bitter is a scornful jest.
SAMUEL JOHNSON

If you miss a putt five inches to the right, he'll come over and say, "Damn, I could have sworn you made that one. You put such a great stroke on it." LEE TREVINO *on Fuzzy Zoeller*

. . .

A cutting or ironic remark is an effortless form of golfmanship for those of us to whom sarcasm comes naturally. But here are some suggestions for the acerbity-challenged:

- Urge your opponent to "Get it close" as he addresses a three-foot putt.
- As your opponent's putt skitters past the cup: "Hit something!" or, "Get in the hole!"
- When your opponent's short putt lips out: "Nice roll!"
- When his fifty-footer stops way short or way long: "Nice lag!"
- Seeing your opponent fan the ball or ground his club in a hazard: "Tough break!" (both to accentuate the negative, and to let him know you saw the infraction).
- Shout, "Snakebit!" when he foolishly tries to hit a miracle shot out of the woods and his ball castanets through the trees, ending up in even worse trouble.

Advanced: On a par-3, as your opponent's shot leaves the clubface, shout "It's in da hole!" in the voice of Bill Murray as greenkeeper Carl in *Caddyshack*. This will have at least two effects: (1) It will give him a millisecond of irrational hope that he has managed to hit a once-in-a-lifetime shot, quickly followed, of course, by disappointment, and (2) it will brand you as either a sarcastic bastard or a lunatic, and thus put him in fear of more such outbursts. (Likewise: "Double-eagle!" on a par-5 as your opponent hits his second shot, though it be clearly off line and a hundred yards short of the green.)

Defense: If your opponent employs sarcasm against you, respond with self-deprecating humor. He who laughs at himself can never be a laughingstock.

CLICHÉ WORK

Golf clichés such as "You drive for show and putt for dough" or "Never up, never in" are extremely annoying, especially after you've just smoked a drive or left a three-foot putt short. In general, mindless repetition of clichés is beneath the dignity of the serious golfman. But there are occasions when the sheer banality of a bromide can unhinge the most tranquil adversary. Just remember that the function of cliché work is to remind your opponent that *someone is rooting against him,* so use them with malice aforethought:

- "On the dance floor, but a long way from the band!" as he lines up his fifty-footer.
- "Nothing rolls like a ball!" as his putt darts ten feet past the cup. (Similarly, the McCordisms: "Full flaps!" or "Grow hair, ball!")
- "Does your husband play?" as he leaves his putt short. (Similarly, "Shorty's in town!")
- "Tote your tapper!" or "There's still some golf left in that one!" when he asks to be given a short putt.

(*Regional variant:* "There's still some chicken left on *that* bone!")

- "Never in doubt!" as his putt circles the hole before falling in the side. (Likewise, "An all-around good putt!")
- "That'll run like a frightened fawn!" when he tops his drive.
- "Every shot pleases someone" as he slices into the woods.
- "A long way the wrong way!" after a long but crooked shot. (Likewise, "Plenty of postage but no address!")
- "Nice wedge!" when he skies a driver.
- "Gainin' on it!" as he skulls an iron twenty yards down the fairway.
- "Better throw a provisional!" after he hurls a club that misses the fairway.
- "You could bury a small dog in that divot," after he chunks one. (An especially disturbing image if your opponent happens to have a Chihuahua. Substitute "kitty" as appropriate.)

If your opponent is prone to a chronic error such as shanking or skulling, adopt a signature exclamation ("D'oh!") for whenever he commits it ("D'oh!"). Repeat it enough and he may imagine he hears it on his backswing ("D'oh!").

An offbeat variation on cliché work involves verbal tics, or the repetition of a word or phrase. I once had a history teacher who was inordinately fond of the phrase "by and large." The class started a pool, with everyone listening carefully for each occurrence, to the exclusion of anything he might have been saying about the subject at hand. I never won the pool (the record: nineteen times in one fifty-minute class), but I did learn a valuable lesson, albeit not about history: Repeat a phrase often enough and it drives out everything else. Try this on your opponent during a round. Even if he doesn't actually count the occurrences, it will wear on him like drops of water torture.

SUGGESTED WORDS AND PHRASES:
- "When the bell rings."
- "At the end of the day."
- "You betcha!"
- "Get over it!"
- "Hopefully."
- "I *hear* ya!"
- "Proactive."
- "Awesome!"
- "*Tell* me about it!"
- "Fuggedaboudit!"
- "Ahm like . . ."

THE CATTLE PROD
· · ·

After Don [January] overtook Miller in one tournament, I said, "Don, you seem to have Miller's number, don't you?" Don grinned. "Mex," he said, "if Miller Barber gets to playing too good, I just take a cattle prod, touch him on the side, and give him a little shock. That takes care of him for the day." LEE TREVINO

. . .

The flamboyant Jimmy Demaret is legendary not only for his great career but also for his on- and off-course antics. He had a stand-up comic's stock of one-liners and a keen sense of timing. For example, when a freak snowstorm hit Pebble Beach during the Crosby, he quipped, "I know I had a few drinks last night, but I didn't expect to wake up in Sun Valley!" But Demaret could turn icy himself when a match was on the line. At a crucial stage, he would flatly tell an opponent: "Go up there and miss that six-footer so I can get to work on this twenty-footer." The key word here (and the cattle prod) being *miss*. The toxic syllable almost always had the desired effect. In a similar vein, Walter Hagen, with a longer putt than his opponent, would announce: "Your putt is going to look a lot longer after I make mine."

Doug Sanders's hideously truncated backswing belied his all-out lifestyle. He was a top money winner and the leading bon vivant on the Tour for several years. Gary Player, on the other hand, was an avid exerciser and clean-liver long before fitness became fashionable. Sanders claimed he could always rattle Player with a simple question before a round: "Are you feeling okay, Gary? You don't look well."

A cattle prod, then, is something the mere utterance of which shocks your opponent. It can be any word, phrase, or sound that upsets him. Cattle prods can be divided into General, Golf-Specific, and Personal. Your selection will be governed by your opponent's handicap, age, state of health, financial condition, etc. A few examples:

GENERAL:	GOLF-SPECIFIC:
accounting irregularities	bunker
biopsy	chunk
cosign	flub
catheter	gag
subpoena	hazard
gingivitis	out of bounds
estate tax	penalty
margin call	shank
erectile dysfunction	stub
	water
	whiff

Personal: Exploit any special vulnerability in your opponent, as when playing against a recent indictee, divorcee, or bankrupt.

Execution: Idly speculate on why so many of golf's miscues begin with the letter "s": "slice," "skull," "snap hook," "shank." Any pretext to reasonably work the baneful words into the conversation will do (you, of course, will have inoculated yourself against these verbal toxins).

A NOTE ON PROFANITY Profanity on the golf course is usually a sign you've lost control. As a conscious tactic, cursing is on a par with Velcro-ripping and change-jingling. But there may be occasions when a well-chosen expletive can work against your opponent without upsetting you, as long as (1) it's out of character for you to use foul language, and (2) it will be sure to offend your opponent (e.g., he's a junior, a Quaker, a member of the clergy, etc.). Otherwise, keep it clean. As Horace Hutchinson noted, "If profanity had an influence on the flight of the ball, the game would be played far better than it is."

THE NEEDLE

"Trash talk" is increasingly common in professional sports. Pro athletes apparently assume that the more obnoxious they are, the more likely their opponent will lose his control trying to teach them a lesson. But trash talk requires a high degree of insensitivity, perhaps even a lack of breeding. Thus for many of us it's repugnant, and hence self-defeating. It also shatters the illusion of camaraderie necessary for the execution of other golfmanship techniques. No, you must sabotage, not bludgeon; tease, not browbeat. You're not launching a frontal assault, you're waging guerilla war. Hence the needle:

. . .

One fine day, Antonio Piñero challenged me to a match, the loser throwing a picnic for a group of friends. . . . I agreed to the challenge.

Antonio brought his psychologist to the match. Every time I tried to give my friend the needle, the psychologist interceded and responded so Antonio felt no pressure. He won the match. ROBERTO DE VICENZO

• • •

The best defense for the needle if you can't bring your psychologist? Ignore it. Block it out. Smile and say nothing. Do not try to retaliate. To be effective, the needle requires give-and-take. That's why Señor Piñero defeated Señor De Vicenzo.

Advanced: A veteran golfman I know loves to brag about the day his needle was so sharp that by the 5th tee, his opponent was literally afraid to speak. The poor devil would not open his mouth for fear of providing another pretext for a devastating verbal assault. But don't expect similar results. Such conversational shell shock has rarely been achieved, and is rightfully considered the Holy Grail of golfmanship.

ADVICE

Gary Player, who has an endorsement deal with Dunlop, asks Ben Hogan, who markets his own line of clubs, for swing advice. Hogan replies, "Why don't you ask Mr. Dunlop?"

The rules of golf prohibit a player from seeking or supplying "advice" during a match, including "any counsel or suggestion which could influence a player in determining his play, the choice of a club or the method of making a stroke." No reply is necessary—merely asking completes the crime. Likewise, if during a round you volunteer that your opponent is overswinging, or gratuitously demonstrate the technique for a given shot, you've committed an infraction punishable by loss of hole in match play or two strokes in medal play.

Therefore, whether you should give advice to your opponent, solicited or unsolicited, will depend on how strictly he adheres to the rule. If he's likely to call you on it, you should of course refrain from giving or asking advice. During a round. Between rounds is another matter. Off-course give-and-take is part of the fellowship of golf. And fertile ground for golfmanship.

Should you ever have the good luck to be asked for advice by an opponent, whether on or off the course, (1) remain calm. Think of yourself as a boxer who has hurt his adversary early in a round. Be patient and deliberate as you go in for the kill, being careful not to "punch yourself out." Wait for an opening to land a haymaker, then, (2) decide whether to take the high road or the low road.

Asked by your opponent for putting advice:

High road: Tell him to "Keep the ball low."

Low road: Tell him to "Hit the ball closer to the hole."

Asked how to play a given shot:

High road: Tell him to "Be sure to pronate."

Low road: Reply, "Play it under an assumed name."

Your opponent proudly displays a new driver:

High road: Admire it, then ask him its swing weight. If he doesn't know, it will make him wonder. If he knows and replies with a number, raise your eyebrows, shake your head, and whistle.

Low road: Ask him if it floats.

Asked by your opponent if there's any trouble on a given hole:

High road: Tell him you make it a practice to avoid all negativity.

Low road: Did he know the course is built on an old Indian burial ground?

Conversely, never "empower" your opponent by genuinely soliciting his advice. But *pretending* to do so will confound him. For instance, ask him how to hit a specific shot—a low punch out of the woods, say. He'll probably describe the technique and be done with it (play the ball back in your stance, move your hands forward, keep your follow-through low, etc.). But, if during a round he is faced with a similar shot, he'll probably use it as an occasion to "demonstrate" his previous advice, and will almost certainly fluff the shot (according to the natural law that turns all demonstrations into misses).

Or, on the practice green just before a round, ask him to "check" your putting grip. It's like tying someone else's tie; the first thing he'll have to do is mentally reverse everything. Confusing.

As Dave Marr stands over a putt during the 1965 PGA Championship at Laurel Valley, he imagines he hears his young son call, "Careful, Daddy, careful!" Marr heeds the disembodied advice and is so careful he three-putts. Fortunately, the voice goes away and Marr eventually wins the championship.

What if your opponent fails to solicit your advice? Tell him to "relax and have fun." (As if it's something he could do voluntarily.) Or, at a crucial point in the match, say when he's faced with a delicate bunker shot, employ the ostensibly well-intentioned "Be careful." It is of course impossible to be careful and hit a decent shot.

THE POWER OF SUGGESTION

. . .

The golfing area of the brain is a fragile thing that is terribly susceptible to suggestion. HARVEY PENICK

. . .

John Cook is making his way to the 72nd hole of the 1983 Tournament Players Championship when an elderly lady in the gallery accosts him, shakes her finger, and says, "Young man, whatever you do, don't hit it in the water!" Cook promptly hooks his tee shot into a lake and makes six on the par-4, dashing his chance to win.

The question of whether it would have been justifiable homicide for Cook to have strangled the old woman is beyond the scope of this book. But the tragic incident illustrates a gamesmanship fundamental: the awesome power of negative suggestion ("Don't throw me in that briar patch"; "Don't think of an elephant"; "Don't mention J. P. Morgan's nose").

VISUALIZATION   There's a popular belief that if you can visualize a good shot, you're more likely to execute one. Many top players use this technique. Before they hit a putt, they "see" the ball going into the hole. Jack Nicklaus says he shows himself a "technicolor movie" of the ball following the desired flight. According to Chi Chi Rodriguez, "your body can only do what your brain sees."

In "associated visualization," you are in the scene. You visually rehearse seeing the ball fly at the target. In "disassociated visualization," you watch yourself on a mental screen making a good shot. In either case, you visualize only the ideal flight of the ball, ignoring all hazards.

Accordingly, if your opponent can be made to visualize a *bad* shot, he's more likely to hit one, so it's up to you to point out all the hazards:

YOU: Well sir, all you have to do is clear the pond (bunker, waste area, quarry, barranca) and you've got it made!

A related gambit involves planting negative suggestions under the guise of seemingly innocent observations:

As Herman Keiser and Byron Nelson approach the green on the 72nd hole of the 1946 Masters, Nelson remarks that Keiser hasn't three-putted all day. Keiser promptly three-putts the green (but hangs on to win the tournament by one shot over Ben Hogan).

· · ·

I came to the final tee three under par for the day, holding a one-stroke lead, needing just par to become the first man in history to win consecutive Masters championships.

Then I simply blew it.

My tee shot was fine, slightly down the left side of the fairway. I walked to my ball feeling really good about the situation. All I had left was a 7-iron approach shot I'd executed dozens of times. As I neared my ball, however, I saw someone at the gallery rope motioning me over. It was none other than my old friend George Low, looking dapper as ever in his jacket and necktie. "Nice going, boy," he said to me, patting my arm affectionately. "You won it."

I made the biggest mistake you can make in such a situation—I accepted the congratulations prematurely and, in doing so, completely destroyed my concentration.

As I stood over the ball, my brain seemed to completely shut down. I was suddenly unsure what I should be thinking about. Instead of seeing nothing around me except the business at hand—which is what any player needing birdie or par to finish and win at Augusta must do—I suddenly seemed to notice everything around me, the color of the sky, the expectant faces of the people in the gallery, you name it. The pin was in its customary Sunday placement, front left, behind the bunker. I remember telling myself to focus only on getting the ball on the green and two-putting. That was where I made my big mistake. As Pap has always sternly advised me in such situations, I should have been thinking only about swinging the club properly and keeping my head still through the impact. Instead, I lifted my head a little and came out of the shot too soon. The ball went right into the bunker.

I compounded that mistake with a worse one. Instead of taking a moment to compose my thoughts and regain my cool, I hurried to the ball and struck an explosive shot that sent it flying out of the sand, across the green, and down a slope toward the television tower. Now, dying inside, I needed to get down in two simply to get into a playoff with Gary [Player]. My fourth shot ran fifteen feet past the hole, and my attempt for bogey failed. I'd double-bogeyed the final hole to lose the Masters by a stroke. ARNOLD PALMER

. . .

Defense: Guard against "rabbit ears," an affliction whereby the victim tunes in to any overheard bits of instruction or casual observations about someone else's swing. (Especially dangerous ground: the practice tee.)

HYPNOSIS Hypnosis is a highly sophisticated technique, the ultimate in opponent management. I do not refer to benign, parlor-trick, you're-a-chicken hypnosis, but to multiple-personality-revealing, past-life-regression hypnosis, which can be a powerful weapon in the hands of an expert. Alas, it is too complex to discuss here, so a basic reading list will have to suffice:

Bernstein, Morey. *The Search for Bridey Murphy* (1956).

Copelan, Rachel. *How to Hypnotize Yourself and Others* (1997).

Hall, James A. *Hypnosis: A Jungian Perspective* (1989).

Lankton, Stephen R. (ed.). *The Broader Implications of Ericksonian Therapy* (1990).

Stockwell, Shelly, et al. *Hypnosis: How to Put a Smile on Your Face and Money in Your Pocket* (1997).

Thigpen, Corbett H. *The Three Faces of Eve* (1957).

Yapko, Michael D. *Trancework: An Introduction to the Practice of Clinical Hypnosis* (1990).

. . .

The first muscle stiffened [in his opponent by the gamesman] is the first point gained. STEPHEN POTTER

. . .

During the 1953 PGA Championship, a gallery member asks Walter Burkemo: "When you address the ball, sometimes you waggle four times and sometimes you waggle five times. How come?" Burkemo doesn't know. He ponders the question for the next three holes, all of which he bogeys.

Likewise, the classic loaded question, "Do you inhale or exhale on the backswing?" is effective because it "makes the unconscious conscious." Which, as Potter well understood, is inimical to the golf swing.

Defense: If anyone ever asks *you* a loaded question, have an answer ready. For example:

HIM: Do you inhale or exhale on your backswing?

YOU: Funny you should ask. David Leadbetter points out that most amateurs get so tense over the ball they neither inhale nor exhale, but rather hold their breath during the swing, depriving the muscles of oxygen and thereby preventing their proper function. Leadbetter suggests whistling softly while swinging, which forces you to breathe out. Similarly, in *The Inner Game of Golf*, Timothy Gallwey recommends humming while swinging. Gary McCord suggests holding a potato chip in your mouth. And the late Gardner Dickinson said he discovered that if you smile or grin during the course of making the stroke, it's almost impossible to be tense or jerky-fast, although he admitted he seldom practiced that way himself because it seemed so silly. Does that answer?

SUGGESTED LOADED QUESTIONS:
- "Do you pull with the left or push with the right?"
- "Do you always hit/tee the ball that high/low?"
- "Which part of the ball do you focus on at address?"
- "Which is your dominant eye?"
- "What's your swing speed?"
- "Are your irons cast or forged?"
- "How much do your shafts weigh?"
- "Why *eighteen* holes?"
- "What, exactly, is the difference between a bal and a blucher?"
- "Does your sunscreen provide UVA *and* UVB protection?"
- "Do you realize you're three-under-fives!?"
- "Do you want me to count that?"

PERMISSION TO FAIL

Always give your opponent permission to fail. If, for example, he's a poor sand player—a probability if he's a mid-to-high-handicapper—tell him about Cary Middlecoff, who won forty tournaments, including two U.S. Opens and a Masters, but who somehow never "got" the explosion shot and often played it like a duffer. As a result, Dr. Middlecoff (the former dentist was "a happy refugee from subgingival curettage," according to Herbert Warren Wind) positively dreaded the sand, whereas most touring pros would prefer to be in a greenside bunker than just short of it—i.e., they'd rather hit an explosion than face a delicate flip over a bunker or a pitch from a bad lie in the grass. The moral for your opponent is clear: He might as well give up trying to improve his sand game if a great player like Middlecoff could never master it.

Another way to give your opponent permission to fail is to reinforce his sense of doom by calling attention to difficult conditions. Bumpy greens, for example, that make putting "impossible" and therefore account for his frequent three-putts. Or "diabolical" pin placements, or "unfair" hole design, or "punitive" rough. What are they trying to *prove?!* You feel his pain, and you're *there* for him.

MUCHMANSHIP

In *The Theory and Practice of Gamesmanship*, Stephen Potter describes a gambit in which you have outdriven your opponent by ten yards, and as you walk together down the fairway and the disparity becomes apparent, you turn to him and say, "Much of a muchness." In other words, you graciously minimize the difference between your drive and his. Which, of course, only reminds him you have outdriven him.

If on the other hand your opponent's drives are consistently longer than yours, don't worry. Allow him to win the battle of the tee shot while you win the war. By driving shorter off the tee, you'll almost certainly be more accurate, and you'll have the advantage of hitting your second shot first—and putting pressure on him.

NATURE BOY

. . .

At a club in my home town there was a golfer . . . who, whenever his opponent or opponents happened to be playing well, would pretend complete lack of interest in the outcome of the match. "How can anyone concentrate on a simply gorgeous day like this?" he would babble in a dreamy cadence. "I just can't take the game seriously when I'm out with you fellows—you're too much fun to be with," he would sigh with affecting wistfulness, or, sometimes, it would be something on the order of "What a fool I am not to play more of these lazy rounds when no one gives a damn if he wins or loses." This fellow would hack away at you with sweet talk until he made you feel like an out-and-out boor for wanting to play your best game. Then, having lulled you into a deep torpor, he would be all business, concede not even an 8-inch putt, become extremely technical about the rules, and relax not for a second until he had the match safely tucked away. HERBERT WARREN WIND

The immensities of space, beside which even polo and baseball are constricted pastimes, must be part of it. To see one's ball gallop two hundred and more yards down the fairway, or see it fly from the face of an 8-iron clear across an entire copse of maples in full autumnal flare, is to join one's soul with the vastness that, contemplated from another angle, intimidates the spirit, and makes one feel small. JOHN UPDIKE

· · ·

Distractions cause mistakes. At crucial stages of the match, call your opponent's attention to the surrounding flora and fauna. For example, pointing out rabbits is very effective, especially if you exclaim, "Look, *bunnies!*" Or ask an endless series of nature-related questions: "What kind of tree is that?" "What kind of grass is that?" "Look at those beautiful cloud formations—are they cirrus, cumulus, or cirrocumulus?" Or pick up a rock, rush over to your opponent, and point out the fine-grained basalt crystals. If you're a guest, ask your opponent/host if there are decent fossils in the local woods.

Intermediate: Sing "My Favorite Things" while waiting together on the tee. If you don't know the lyrics, fancy whistling is also effective. Extra credit for yodeling.

Advanced: When you're two down on the back nine, look around you in wonderment, lean over to your opponent and whisper in his ear: "All this beautiful space devoted to . . . a *game!* It makes one giddy!"

WATER WORK

. . .

Water creates a neurosis in golfers. The very thought of this harmless fluid robs them of their normal powers of rational thought, turns their legs to jelly, and produces a palsy of the upper limbs. PETER DOBEREINER

. . .

Water hazards terrify most golfers, and no wonder: They involve golf's equivalent of capital punishment, with the double retribution of a penalty stroke and the loss of a ball. You must therefore do everything you can to subtly encourage your opponent to hit into the water, and then take full advantage when he does.

When your opponent faces a shot over a water hazard, quote Bobby Jones: "The difference between a sand bunker and water is the difference between a car crash and an airplane crash. You have a chance of recovering from a car crash." Or tell him you heard that last year divers took over seventeen thousand balls out of this very hazard. After your opponent has hit into the water:

High road: Keep quiet and let the shot eat away at his morale. The silence in such circumstances can be deafening. Remember, unless it's a lateral hazard, he'll probably have to negotiate the water again, often from a "drop area" closer to the hole—an even more delicate shot.

Low road: Repeat one of the many colorful but irritating euphemisms for a water ball: "bass bait," "duck humper," "Duncan Hines" (the ball is "moist"), "stogie soaker," "Luca Brasi" (the ball "sleeps with the fishes"), "mushee," "scuba diver," "watery grave," etc.

THE HAIL MARY

Near the end of a round in which you're taking a thrashing—say you're three-down with four to play—step up to your opponent, shake his hand, and say, "You really played well today." Maybe it will convince him the match is already over.

THE ZONE

. . .

The zone is the ability to give 110 percent of your attention and your focus to the shot. When I'm on the tee, I'll see a divot in the fairway and try to run my ball over that divot—and succeed. That's the zone. NICK PRICE

. . .

"The Zone" is the term for a dreamlike state of athletic grace in which you can do no wrong. Your drives roll an extra twenty yards down the center of the fairway, your irons are crisp, and your putts drop from everywhere. Yes, the Zone is rare. But disastrous if your opponent is in it, which is why you must snap him out of it immediately:

Low road: "Man, you're in the *Zone!* You can do no *wrong!* You can swing *as hard as you want today!*"

High road: There is no high road when your opponent is in the Zone.

PART VII

EQUIPMENT WORK

A WORKMAN'S TOOLS

· · ·

Golf clubs aren't only tools. They're totems. The game turns on illusions. FRANK HANNIGAN

From an engineering standpoint, we've designed these irons [Great Big Bertha Tungsten Titanium Irons] in such a way that they don't *want* to slice or fade; don't *want* to dig in the rough; don't *want* to flutter in sand.
CALLAWAY GOLF PRODUCTS BROCHURE (*italics theirs*)

· · ·

The standard equipment ploy is a two-pronged assault: (1) praise yours, and (2) denigrate his. Credit your clubs whenever you hit a good shot. Talk about your "pet" driver and your "sweetheart" putter. Mention the scary moment you thought you'd lost your trusty sand wedge. Your opponent will soon wonder why *he* never had such a close relationship with *his* sand wedge. On a cold day, tell him 100-compression balls get rock-hard below 58 degrees Fahrenheit (a myth, actually), or that graphite shafts lose 2 percent of their flexibility for every degree of temperature under 55 (even if he doesn't buy it, he'll be doing the arithmetic instead of thinking about his game). In a somewhat more risky but potentially devastating gambit, hint that your own equipment is illegal (but never admit any wrongdoing).

By the same natural law that insures you will choose the

slowest checkout line at the supermarket, the other guy's gear always looks better. Though we all have access to the same equipment, the other guy's always seems state-of-the-art, while our own stuff, after bitter experience, seems woefully inadequate. Indeed, it's only human to suspect that faults lie not in ourselves but in our implements. Cultivate this doubt in your opponent with simple questions: Are his shafts too firm (or soft) for his swing speed? Are his irons too upright (or flat)? Are his grips perhaps a thirty-second too small (or large)? Does his glove fit properly?

Ask him if his clubs are custom-fitted. If he says no, smile and shake your head. If he says yes, ask him if they were fitted *outdoors*. Explain that a competent clubfitter needs to see the flight of the ball to develop an accurate set of specs. In a more direct approach, examine your opponent's new driver and snicker, or make a few strokes with his putter and ask, "You *putt* with this?"

An offbeat but valuable equipment ploy involves footwear. If your opponent is wearing Softspikes and you're not, ask him if he thinks they give him "enough traction." If you're wearing Softspikes and he's not, tell him you switched "out of fairness."

PARALYSIS THROUGH ANALYSIS

The British call it "baffling oneself with science." We all know at least one equipment hound, someone who's constantly tinkering and theorizing and making small (read: imaginary) adjustments to his equipment. A clubfitter I know tells of a customer who spent three hours discussing various shaft options in the most arcane terms, including "torque," "frequency" "kick point," etc. Just before the clubfitter finally managed to extricate himself from the conversation, he couldn't resist asking the customer his handicap. "Well, I don't actually have a handicap," the man replied, "but I average a hundred and two."

Moral: Unless you're a low-handicapper, avoid such time-wasting, energy-sapping, ultimately futile equipment-tweaking. And, of course, encourage it in your opponent. If he's obliging enough to confuse himself, why stand in his way?

THE ANALS OF GOLF

. . .

Never play golf with a guy who has one of those bags with separate compartments for all of the irons. Each club will have to be soaked, rinsed, dried and polished after he uses it. And it will have to be stored in the proper sequence. A 7-iron gets in the wrong compartment, there goes a half-hour. DAN JENKINS

. . .

You know the type: Guys who have plastic covers for their irons, or a rack that arrays the clubs in order. Guys who wear tee holsters on their belts. Guys who carry a moistened towel onto the green. These "anals" are so easily rattled it's almost pitiable. Anything that disturbs their rigid sense of order will hurt their game, so be creative. Ask to borrow your opponent's driver (they hate to share). Pretend to test the shaft by pressing the clubhead into the ground (it's harmless but looks bad). Or hide one of his headcovers in an obscure compartment of his own bag.

Advanced: Without asking permission, pull one of his clubs, waggle it several times, covertly smear sunscreen on the grip, then replace it in the wrong compartment.

MAGNETS

Some golfers swear by magnets. They wrap themselves in magnet girdles, fasten magnets to various parts of their bodies with Velcro, wear golf shoes with built-in magnets, even sleep on magnet pads. Magnets are especially popular among older golfers, and they're ubiquitous on the Senior PGA Tour. Do magnets really work? One claim is that they increase blood flow, which decreases pain and promotes healing. Another is that they raise the body's endorphin level. Still another says they combat "electromagnetic pollution" from televisions, computers, and cell phones that impairs the body's natural ability to heal itself. But there's little scientific evidence to support any of these claims. There's no proof to the contrary, either.

Magnets are just the latest in a series of putative cures for golf-related infirmities—copper bracelets for arthritic wrists have been popular for decades. If these remedies are perceived to work, it may be due to the "placebo effect," the physical benefit of positive expectations. Well, the placebo effect is a two-edged sword. Thus, you introduce to your magnet- or bracelet-wearing opponent the "nocebo" effect, the physical manifestation of pessimism, the consequences of disbelief, *the power of negative thinking.* You undermine his confidence in whatever medical talisman he believes in. Has he heard about the laboratory mice who developed cancer after wearing magnets? Did he read the Surgeon General's report on the possible connection between copper bracelets and impotence? (And while you're at it, did he know that Advil is addictive?)

CARTMANSHIP

Though some view it as a blight on the game, the motorized golf cart has enabled millions to play who would not otherwise venture onto a golf course. Carts provide extra revenue for margin-squeezed golf operations, and they're indispensable at the increasing number of courses where caddies are not available. So, whatever we may think of them, carts are here to stay. And they're a rich source of gambits and ploys. But be forewarned: Cartmanship is hard-core, the slapstick of golfmanship, which is to say it requires a warped mind and a nimble body.

The first rule of cartmanship: Always take the wheel. Then you can literally drive your opponent to distraction. (*Caution:* If your opponent won't relinquish the driver's seat, insist on separate carts or . . . walk!) Once you've secured the wheel, you can relax and be a benevolent despot most of the time, driving smoothly and considerately. But when you need help on the scorecard, turn the cart into an instrument of torture: Fumble with the key. Set and reset the brake. Barrel down the fairway pretending not to see a sprinkler head or yardage marker, then swerve at the last instant. (If he complains, call him an "old lady" or a "Nervous Nellie"—feminization of a male opponent is surefire.)

Brake for imaginary obstacles. When you reach his ball, give him a "false stop," i.e., just as he is about to step out of the cart, roll another few yards past his ball, then insist on driving him back. After he has dismounted and is rummaging in his bag for a club, suddenly hit the accelerator. If you're lucky, he'll be grasping a tentative choice just as the cart lurches for-

1.

CARTMANSHIP: 1. As your opponent rummages for a club:
2. Suddenly hit the accelerator. If you're lucky, he'll be grasping a
tentative choice just as the cart lurches forward, which will have
the effect of your choosing for him. 3. Once he has club in hand,
speed away before he can change his mind.

ward, which will have the effect of your choosing the club for him. (Try this only if your opponent's clubbing instincts are sound—wouldn't want to inadvertently help a bad clubber.) This will rattle him, and in rare cases, may even cause him to break a shaft. (Apologize profusely.) Once he has a club in hand, don't dawdle—speed away before he can change his mind. After he hits his shot and you come back to pick him up, floor it just as he attempts to sit down.

And then there's the cartmanship version of the Rolling Start (which see): Pop the brake just as your opponent reaches the top of his backswing. Or slip the cart into reverse while he's over his ball (assuming the cart is equipped with a backup alarm).

Intermediate: If you're two down on the back nine, run over your opponent's ball.

Advanced: While your opponent's attention is elsewhere, quietly unbuckle the strap holding his bag to the cart. When the cart moves forward and the bag falls off, pretend not to notice. Many would say that such a puerile tactic would never be countenanced by an adult, let alone an accomplished golf-man, and *I myself* have never tried it.

PART VIII

. . . . .

TERMINOLOGY

"GOLF" IS NOT A VERB

Golf talk is a sort of Esperanto. Golfers all over the world speak the same language, with its own rules of grammar and usage. And just as speech reveals breeding, golf talk reveals skill level. For example, you'll seldom hear a good player use "golf" as a verb. Pros and low-handicappers don't *golf,* they *play* golf. (*Exception:* In some circles, it is said: "He can really *golf* his ball." But these are the same people who say, "I really hit it good today." Pass.)

To be an effective golfman, avoid golf solecisms, because it's hard to dominate an opponent who finds you ridiculous. Conversely, if you know the jargon, it will brand you one of the cognoscenti, no matter how high your handicap. Yes, you can talk the talk even if you can't walk the walk. Indeed, if you can talk the talk, you may not *need* to walk the walk. You can intimidate your opponent with obscure golf terms. Why? Because jargon is exclusionary. Judicious use of it will make your opponent uneasy, since he'll probably have heard the terms before, but he'll almost certainly have no idea what they mean. Here then, a glossary of golf arcana to perplex your opponent:

GLOSSARY

angle of approach—the angle at which the clubhead meets the ball, measured in degrees.

bend point—the point of maximum bend on a shaft when both ends are compressed. Cf. *flex point, kick point.*

beta titanium—a titanium alloy harder and stronger than the more common 6-4 Ti alloy.

bisque—a handicap stroke that may be applied at the discretion of the recipient.

blade—a forged iron.

bounce—the downward angle of the bottom or sole of the clubhead from front to back. The greater the angle, the greater the bounce.

bulge—the horizontal curvature of the face of a wood.

burn—Scottish for "stream."

cast irons—irons made in molds.

center of gravity—the point in a clubhead where its weight is concentrated.

center-shafted—a putter in which the shaft is attached to the center of the clubhead.

compression—the amount a ball is flattened on impact with the clubhead, determined by core hardness. Compression affects feel, but not distance.

custom grind—customized irons, especially forged blades, favored by tour players. Custom grinding involves adding or removing material to or from the clubhead to change *swing-weight* or appearance.

dormie—in match play, the state of being x holes up with x holes to play.

double cover—a ball with a solid core, an inner layer, and an outer cover (designed for soft feel).

dwell time—the amount of time the ball is in contact with a putterface during the stroke, measured in microseconds. The greater the dwell time, the more topspin, less skid, and hence truer roll.

face-balanced—a putter whose shaft is positioned through its *center of gravity* so its face stays parallel to the ground when balanced by the shaft. Face-balancing helps keep the putterhead square through the stroke. Cf. *toe-down*.

firth—Scottish for a narrow inlet from the sea.

flex point—the point of maximum bend on a shaft when the tip is deflected. The lower the flex point, the higher the ball trajectory. Synonymous with *kick point*.

foozle—(verb) to flub a shot; (noun) a flubbed shot.

forged irons—irons made one at a time from a solid block of metal.

forgiveness—margin for error on a mishit.

frequency—a measure of the stiffness of a shaft.

gear effect—the spin created by the conjunction of the face of the club and the angle at which the ball is struck.

gorse—spiny green shrubs found on linksland courses.

hanging lie—a situation in which the ball is above your feet, i.e., on the side of a hill.

hogback—a ridge on a green or fairway.

hosel—the part of a clubhead that connects with the shaft.

insert—material in the face of a putter made of rubber, elastomer, teryllium, tungsten, copper, etc., to soften "feel" and increase *dwell time*.

kick point—the point of maximum bend on a shaft when

the tip is deflected. The lower the kick point, the higher the ball trajectory. Synonymous with *flex point*.

kiltie—a fringed leather flap covering the laces of a golf shoe.

laid off—a swing flaw in which the clubface points at the sky at the top of the backswing.

lie angle—the angle between the shaft and the ground at address, measured in degrees. If the heel is raised, the lie angle is "flat." If the toe is raised, the lie angle is "upright."

low-profile—a club, usually a fairway wood, with low clubface height, such as Orlimar's TriMetal or Adams Tight Lies. Synonymous with *shallow-face*.

maraging steel—an extremely hard and strong stainless steel alloy used in clubheads, especially as face *inserts*.

modulus—a measure of the purity of a graphite shaft. The higher the modulus, the stronger the shaft.

offset—a design in which the shaft and *hosel* are positioned ahead of the clubface to help the hands get through the hitting area and thereby prevent slicing.

perimeter weighting—a design in which weight is distributed around the periphery of the clubhead to make it more *forgiving* on off-center hits.

roll—the vertical curvature of the face of a wood.

rota—the circuit of courses where the British Open is played, including the Old Course at St. Andrews, Royal Troon, Carnoustie, the Ailsa Course at Turnberry, Muirfield, and others.

sclaff—to hit the ground before the ball, i.e., to "drop-kick" it.

set configuration—the mix of fourteen clubs in a bag at a given time, which might change with playing conditions.

shallow-face—a club, usually a fairway wood, with low clubface height, such as Orlimar's TriMetal or Adams Tight Lies. Synonymous with *low-profile*.

slope system—a method of rating golf courses according to difficulty, to adjust handicaps.

static weight—the overall weight of a club.

Stimpmeter—a device for measuring the speed of greens.

Surlyn—a tough resin made by DuPont used to make 90 percent of modern golf ball covers.

sweet spot—the absolute center of a clubface. There is no vertical or horizontal rotation of the clubhead when the ball is struck on the sweet spot.

swing plane—the angle at which the club travels around the body.

swingweight—the weight of the clubhead, grip, and shaft in relation to one another. The addition of two grams to a clubhead increases swingweight one point (e.g., D-1 to D-2).

three-piece wound—a ball with a solid or liquid core wrapped in rubber thread with a soft cover (designed for spin).

toe-down—a toe-down putter is not *face-balanced*, i.e., the centerline is in the heel.

topline—the top edge of an iron (viewed at address). A thick topline increases the club's effective loft, making it easier to get the ball airborne.

torque—the rotational twisting of a shaft upon impact, expressed in degrees.

two-piece—a ball with a solid core and a durable outer cover (designed for distance).

whins—*gorse* bushes.

It's particularly bothersome to play with someone who insists on calling clubs by their old Scottish names. Hence you may want to call clubs by their old Scottish names:

baffing spoon—a short-shafted, steeply lofted wooden club used for approach shots.

baffy—four-wood.

brassie—two-wood.

cleek—one-iron.

jigger—a lofted iron used for pitching.

mashie—five-iron.

mashie-niblick—seven-iron.

mid-iron—two-iron.

mid-mashie—three-iron.

niblick—nine-iron.

pitching-niblick—eight-iron.

spade-mashie—six-iron.

spoon—three-wood.

USAGE NOTES

Some golf announcers refer to members of the same group in Tour events as "playing *partners*." Avoid this common conceptual error. No matter how ostensibly convivial the atmosphere, you're there to win, not to socialize, and you're playing *against* an adversary, not *with* a partner. Even if your opponent is your brother, he's your enemy on the course and should be given no quarter, except in the execution of some gambit.

Likewise, I wince whenever a commentator says that so-and-so made a "courageous putt." For me a putt would be courageous if the green were mined, or there were Cape buffalo roaming the course, or if the stroke were attempted under extreme duress:

> With four holes to play in the final round of the 1977 U.S. Open, Hubert Green is informed of a death threat against him. He is given three options: He can continue playing with a police escort, he can suspend play, or he can withdraw from the tournament. He chooses to continue, jokes that the threat probably came from an ex-girlfriend, and promptly pars in to win his first and only U.S. Open.

Threats of physical violence from the gallery aside, there's nothing in a game of golf important enough to elevate a given stroke to "courageous" status. "Gritty" maybe. It takes grit to play championship golf. Not the same grit it takes to play rugby, say, but mental toughness, a much rarer commodity than physical courage. Which is why a psychological guerilla fighter has a tremendous edge.

AFTERWORD

. . .

Pure play and unquestioned excellence is the death of technique. Against the bravest opposition, merit and sportsmanship emasculates the gambit and nullifies the ploy. STEPHEN POTTER

. . .

Potter was referring to Bobby Jones, and though there was only one Bobby Jones, be advised that even master gamesmen are occasionally outclassed. For example, in the final round of the 1974 Glen Campbell–Los Angeles Open at Riviera, sixty-one-year-old Sam Snead and thirty-two-year-old Dave Stockton arrived at the 17th hole in a tight battle for the lead. Here's Stockton's account of what happened next:

At 17, we both had a little over 100 yards left for our third shots, and Sam hit first. He put his shot pin-high about 10 feet away, and he started walking ahead of me. At first I thought he was walking ahead to get his divot, but he just kept going all the way to the green and making me wait. Then he marked his ball and stood just a little bit to the side. I knew what he was doing and I was furious. I hit my ball on the green and made par, but Sam sank his putt so my lead was only one.

On the 18th tee we had to wait a bit. Sam said something like, "You know, I birdied the last two holes here once to beat Hogan." The wind was against us and Sam got up and bombed a perfect drive. I pulled mine a bit, and it got caught in the sidehill rough. I had 243 yards to the pin. Luckily my lie was extremely good, so I decided to go with a 3-wood.

I got ready to play my shot, and Sam's standing right there beside my caddie—so close he's almost inside my golf bag. I can't tell you how mad I was by this point. But somehow I just killed this 3-wood, and it ran up about 12 feet from the hole. And right there with the TV cameras and all, I pumped my fist under Sam's nose and told him, "I'll bet Hogan didn't hit it that close!" I wound up winning by two. Over the years I've gone back to that same spot and tried that shot over again at least 20 times, and I haven't hit the green even once.

If you've ever competed against someone who got the ball up and down from everywhere, or hit green after green in regulation, or sank every putt he looked at, you'll understand that, unfortunately, pure play beats golfmanship every time. Fortunately, pure play is extremely rare.

ACKNOWLEDGMENTS

I'm grateful to the civilians: Kent Barton, Norrie Epstein, Archie Ferguson, Diana Secker Larson, LuAnn Walther, Elinor Winokur, and to the golfers: Jeff Benninghofen, Reid Boates, Paul Bogaards, Jim Detrixhe, Don Duber, James Garner, Gary McCord, Mike Miller, Norm Wiles, and Millie Zimring. I'm especially indebted to Sam Williams for countless contributions to this book, and for encouraging my return to the game.

INDEX